WHAT MY CPA SHOULD HAVE TOLD ME

BEFORE

40

AF867605

The C.A.T. Method for Cash Flow, Assets, and Tax Planning in Every Quarter of Life

Busayo Ogunsanya, CPA, MST

Before 40 Club

This book is for education, not for individualized advice. It provides general information about tax, financial, and legal topics, and none of it constitutes tax, legal, investment, or accounting advice for your specific situation. Tax laws change, thresholds move, and your facts are your own. Before acting on anything in this book, consult a qualified professional who can see your actual numbers. Client scenarios described in this book are composites, anonymized, or used with permission.

Published by Before 40 Club, New York
before40club.com

DEDICATION

To the memory of my father, Babatunde Ogunsanya.

He ran his own businesses his whole life, veterinary medicine, fumigation, whatever the season asked of him, and he made sure his children knew that ownership was normal. Everything in this book about building something of your own, I learned first by watching him.

I wish he were here to hold this.

Table of Contents

INTRODUCTION: 1

WELCOME TO THE CLUB 1

I Passed the Exam. Then the Real Education Began 2

THE GAME 7

CHAPTER 1: 8

The Expensive Lesson 8

The Story 9

What Nobody Told You 10

The C.A.T. Breakdown 12

The Quarter Lens 13

A Note if You Are Past 40 14

The Move to Make Now 14

The Warning 15

The Checklist 15

The Before 40 Club Rule 16

CHAPTER 2: 17

The Expensive Lesson 17

The Story 18

What Nobody Told You 19

The C.A.T. Breakdown 20

The Quarter Lens 21

The Move to Make Now 21

The Warning 22

The Checklist 22

The Before 40 Club Rule 23

CHAPTER 3: 24

The Expensive Lesson 24

The Story 25
What Nobody Told You 25
The C.A.T. Breakdown 28
The Quarter Lens 30
Health Through C.A.T. 31
The Move to Make Now 31
The Warning 32
The Checklist 32
The Before 40 Club Rule 32
CHAPTER 4: 33
The Expensive Lesson 33
The Story 34
What Nobody Told You 34
The C.A.T. Breakdown 36
The Quarter Lens 37
The Debt Layer: Cash Flow's Shadow 38
The Move to Make Now 39
The Warning 39
The Checklist 39
The Before 40 Club Rule 40
CHAPTER 5: 41
The Expensive Lesson 41
The Story 42
What Nobody Told You 42
The C.A.T. Breakdown 44
The Quarter Lens 45
The Move to Make Now 46
The Warning 46
The Checklist 47

The Before 40 Club Rule 47
CHAPTER 6: 48
The Expensive Lesson 48
The Story 49
What Nobody Told You 50
The C.A.T. Breakdown 51
The Quarter Lens 52
The Move to Make Now 53
The Warning 53
The Checklist 54
The Before 40 Club Rule 54
PART II: 55
THE EXAMS 55
CHAPTER 7: 56
The Expensive Lesson 56
The Story 57
What Nobody Told You 58
The C.A.T. Breakdown 60
The Quarter Lens 61
The Move to Make Now 62
The Warning 62
The Checklist 63
The Before 40 Club Rule 63
CHAPTER 8: 64
The Expensive Lesson 64
The Story 65
What Nobody Told You 65
The C.A.T. Breakdown 68
The Quarter Lens 69

The Move to Make Now 70
The Warning 70
The Checklist 71
The Before 40 Club Rule 71
CHAPTER 9: 72
The Expensive Lesson 72
The Story 73
What Nobody Told You 74
C.A.T. for Kids: Start at Five 76
The C.A.T. Breakdown 77
The Quarter Lens 77
The Move to Make Now 78
The Warning 78
The Checklist 79
The Before 40 Club Rule 79
CHAPTER 10: 80
The Expensive Lesson 80
The Story 81
What Nobody Told You 82
The C.A.T. Breakdown 84
The Quarter Lens 85
The Move to Make Now 85
The Warning 86
The Checklist 87
The Before 40 Club Rule 87
CHAPTER 11: 88
The Expensive Lesson 88
The Story 89
What Nobody Told You 90

The C.A.T. Breakdown 92
The Quarter Lens 92
The Move to Make Now 93
The Warning 93
The Checklist 94
The Before 40 Club Rule 94
CHAPTER 12: 96
The Expensive Lesson 96
The Story 97
What Nobody Told You 97
The C.A.T. Breakdown 100
The Quarter Lens 101
The Move to Make Now 101
The Warning 102
The Checklist 103
The Before 40 Club Rule 103
CHAPTER 13: 104
The Expensive Lesson 104
The Story 105
What Nobody Told You 106
The C.A.T. Breakdown 108
The Quarter Lens 109
The Move to Make Now 110
The Warning 111
The Checklist 111
The Before 40 Club Rule 112
CHAPTER 14: 113
The Expensive Lesson 113
The Story 114

What Nobody Told You 114
The C.A.T. Breakdown 117
The Quarter Lens 118
The Move to Make Now 119
The Warning 119
The Checklist 120
The Before 40 Club Rule 120
CHAPTER 15: 121
The Expensive Lesson 121
The Story 122
What Nobody Told You 123
The C.A.T. Breakdown 126
The Quarter Lens 127
The Move to Make Now 127
The Warning 128
The Checklist 129
The Before 40 Club Rule 129
PART III: 130
THE PLAYER 130
CHAPTER 16: 131
The Expensive Lesson 131
The Story 132
What Nobody Told You 133
The C.A.T. Breakdown 135
The Quarter Lens 136
The Move to Make Now 137
The Warning 137
The Checklist 138
The Before 40 Club Rule 138

CHAPTER 17: 140
The Expensive Lesson 140
The Story 141
What Nobody Told You 142
The C.A.T. Breakdown 144
The Quarter Lens 145
The Move to Make Now 146
The Warning 146
The Checklist 147
The Before 40 Club Rule 147
CHAPTER 18: 149
The Expensive Lesson 149
The Story 150
What Nobody Told You 151
The C.A.T. Breakdown 154
The Quarter Lens 155
The Move to Make Now 156
The Warning 157
The Checklist 157
The Before 40 Club Rule 158
CHAPTER 19: 159
The Expensive Lesson 159
The Story 160
What Nobody Told You 161
The C.A.T. Breakdown 163
The Quarter Lens 164
The Move to Make Now 164
The Warning 165
The Checklist 165

The Before 40 Club Rule 166
CHAPTER 20: 167
The Expensive Lesson 167
The Story 168
What Nobody Told You 169
The C.A.T. Breakdown 172
The Quarter Lens 173
The Move to Make Now 173
The Warning 174
The Checklist 174
The Before 40 Club Rule 174
PART IV: 176
THE ENDGAME 176
CHAPTER 21: 177
The Expensive Lesson 177
The Story 178
What Nobody Told You 179
The C.A.T. Breakdown 181
The Quarter Lens 182
The Move to Make Now 183
The Warning 183
The Checklist 184
The Before 40 Club Rule 184
CHAPTER 22: 185
The Expensive Lesson 185
The Story 186
What Nobody Told You 186
The C.A.T. Breakdown 188
The Quarter Lens 189

The Move to Make Now 190
The Warning 191
The Checklist 191
The Before 40 Club Rule 191
CHAPTER 23: 193
The Expensive Lesson 193
The Story 194
What Nobody Told You 195
The C.A.T. Breakdown 197
The Quarter Lens 198
Executive Time: Divide Your Days by RGA 199
The Health Layer: The Asset Under Everything 200
The Move to Make Now 202
The Warning 202
The Checklist 203
The Before 40 Club Rule 203
OVERTIME: THE LAST QUARTER IS DECIDED NOW 204
JOINING THE BEFORE 40 CLUB 207
APPENDIX: THE BEFORE 40 CLUB DICTIONARY 208
The Vocabulary 208
The Compounding Laws 210
The 23 Rules 211
ABOUT THE AUTHOR 214
Where to Find Me 214

INTRODUCTION: WELCOME TO THE CLUB

Somebody should have told you.

That is the sentence underneath every page of this book, and it is the sentence underneath most of the money pain I have witnessed in 18 years as a CPA. Somebody should have told you what a W-4 actually controls before your first paycheck. Somebody should have told you what an LLC does and does not do before you paid a website to form one. Somebody should have told you about the five-year clock before you started the company, the true monthly cost before you bought the house, the merger before the wedding, the step-up in basis before the family moved the deed, the four things to check before you paid that notice. Somebody should have told you, and nobody did, and so you learned the way almost everyone learns money in this country: the expensive way, one surprise invoice at a time, with the tuition compounding quietly in the background.

I wrote this book to be the somebody.

My name is Busayo Ogunsanya. I am a Certified Public Accountant with a Master's degree in Taxation, and for 18 years I have worked across tax, accounting, startups, and the real money problems of real people: business owners, physicians, founders, high earners, first-generation builders, and families holding one scary envelope. I have written six books on tax before this one. I have run my own firm, built my own company, sat on the founder's side of the table and the CPA's side of the same table, sometimes in the same week. And across all of it, one experience repeats so reliably that I finally organized my whole working life around it: the person across the desk was never stupid. They were untaught, and the gap between untaught and taught was costing them more than any market crash ever would.

This book exists because of a pattern I could not stop seeing. I have been a CPA for 18 years. I hold a master's in taxation. I have started multiple companies and scaled my own businesses to seven figures. And across all of it, I have sat with everyone from low-income filers to multimillionaires, and clients whose exits ran to eight and nine figures, and read the one document where every financial life tells the truth: the return.

Meet enough clients across enough seasons and the pattern names itself. The people who win are running the same three-part play, whether they know it or not. Look at how LeBron James operates: enormous cash flow, converted deliberately into assets, the equity deals, the ownership stakes, the tequila company, the sports franchises, all of it wrapped in structure. Then look at the high earner in corporate America making seven hundred thousand dollars in W-2 income plus stock grants, and notice that every single component of that compensation has a tax consequence attached, whether or not anyone ever explained it to them. Cash flow. Assets. Tax planning. If nobody tells you about these three, you will spend your whole life scratching your head at how other people make and keep their capital. Somebody who reads the returns for a living is now telling you. That is the entire reason this book exists.

I Passed the Exam. Then the Real Education Began

There is a joke in my profession that CPA stands for Can't Pass Again, because the exam is a monster and nobody who survives it wants a rematch. I passed it while working full time. I added a master's in taxation on top, riding the train to Fordham at night. And I want to be precise about what all that education actually gave me, because the precision is the point of this section: the credentials taught me discipline, technical ability, preparation, accuracy, and how to operate under pressure. Those are real, they are rare, and they built the professional the rest of this book leans on.

Here is what they did not teach me, and I only found out when I branched out and started building my own ventures: sales. Product. Distribution. Leadership. Marketing. Negotiation. Managing my own cash flow instead of auditing someone else's. Managing my time when nobody was assigning it. Personal branding. Resilience. Ownership. And my own health, which it took me embarrassingly long to recognize as part of the curriculum at all. School taught me how to qualify for an opportunity. Building my own things taught me how to create one. Passing the CPA exam proved I could master difficult information. Branching out on my own taught me how to master myself.

Understand what I am not saying. This is not an anti-school book and it is not an anti-job book, and it cannot be, because Chapter 18 will show you employees operating with more ownership than some founders, and because employees absolutely become millionaires through strong income, equity, disciplined investing, and compounding. The lesson is narrower and more useful: professional excellence prepares you to be a strong player inside an existing system. Nobody hands you the course on building the system, designing the life, or running the machine that is you. That course is self-enrolled, and this book is my version of the syllabus.

Two words run underneath everything that follows, so let me define them here and you will feel them in every chapter. Agency is the belief that your choices, your preparation, your habits, your conversations, your relationships, and your calendar can meaningfully change the direction of your life. Urgency is the recognition that time is limited and that delayed decisions quietly convert into financial, professional, relational, and health consequences. Urgency is not panic and it is not recklessness. It is the refusal to live indefinitely in avoidance. Agency says, I can do something about this. Urgency says, I should not keep waiting. Agency without urgency becomes potential. Urgency without agency becomes anxiety. You need both, and this book is designed to install both.

And one warning that the rest of the book will keep proving: if you do not curate your life, your obligations, your distractions, your habits, and other people's priorities will curate it for you. Your calendar, your cash flow, your career, your health, your relationships, your home, your weekends, your information diet, your reputation, your future. Every one of those is being curated right now, by you or by default. The method you are about to learn is, at bottom, a curation system, and money is simply where we start.

So let me tell you what this book is, what it is not, and how to use it.

The promise, in one line: stop learning money lessons the expensive way. Every chapter in this book exists because somewhere, someone paid full price for its absence, usually in front of me, usually years after the cheap version was available. The book's entire job is to move you from the group that finds out after to the group that decided before. Before the marriage, before the house, before the business, before the letter, before the exit, before 40. The word before is doing all the work in this book's title, and it will do all the work in your results.

The method, in three letters: C.A.T. Cash Flow, Assets, Tax Planning. Master your cash flow, buy the right assets, and plan your taxes around both. That is the whole game, and Chapter 3 is the full sermon. Every money decision you will ever face runs through those three letters, and by the end of this book, running them will be a reflex that fires in dealerships, open houses, offer letters, and family conversations, whether I am there or not. That is the goal. I am trying to install something, not just explain something.

The clock, in five quarters. Your money life runs like a game: Q1, ages 0 to 21, when your defaults got installed without your permission. Q2, 21 to 40, the build quarter, when time is your biggest asset and every move compounds longest. Q3, 41 to 60, the accelerate quarter, when the presence or absence of a system becomes impossible to hide. Q4, 61 to 80, the protect quarter. And Overtime, 80 and beyond, when everything either transfers on purpose or dissolves by default. Knowing which quarter you are in changes what the right move is, and every chapter ends by turning its lesson through all five.

And one thing settled right here, because the name on the cover raises it: **the Before 40 Club is not about your age.** It is about the decision to stop learning money lessons the expensive way. Some join at 28. Some join at 52 wishing they joined at 28. Both are welcome. Only one waited. If you are reading this at 45 or 55, nothing in this book is closed to you, the sequence is identical and the runway is shorter, which makes the decision more urgent, not less available. The title is a deadline for the people who still have it and a door for everyone who does not.

Now, what this book is not, because I want us honest with each other from page one.

This is not a textbook, and I have worked hard to make sure it never sounds like one. This is not generic financial literacy content, the kind that explains compound interest with a smiling stock photo and changes nothing. This is not a get-rich system, a market-timing scheme, or a collection of loopholes; you will find, in fact, that this book is openly hostile to loopholes, because I have spent 18 years watching loopholes convert into penalty notices. And critically: this book is not personalized advice. I do not know your numbers, your state, your entity, or your family, and the tax code cares about all four. This book teaches frameworks, the questions, the sequences, the rules of the game. The specific answer for your specific situation is a conversation with a professional who can see your actual return, and one of this book's recurring jobs is teaching you how to find, hire, and use that person properly. The framework is the book. The personalized answer is the reason professionals exist.

What this book also is not: clean. There is a chapter near the end called The Goofball Chapter, and it is the chapter most money books skip, the one about the wrong friends, the wrong partners, the ego purchases, the oversharing, the expensive decisions that felt completely reasonable at the time. It is in this book because after 18 years I can tell you that most money mistakes are not math mistakes. They are people mistakes and ego mistakes wearing a math costume, and a book that only teaches the math is only teaching half the game. I go first in that chapter. It seemed only fair.

A few words on how to read this thing.

The book runs in four parts. **Part One, The Game,** builds the foundation: the rules nobody taught you, the audit of where your defaults came from, the C.A.T. Method in full, and the deep chapters on each letter, cash flow, assets, and tax planning. Read Part One in order, because each chapter sizes the next. **Part Two, The Exams,** takes the method into the real-life events where money is actually won and lost: marriage, the house, kids, the business, the IRS letter, the high-earner years, family money, the rental, and equity. Those chapters stand alone; if there is a wedding or a closing on your calendar, skip ahead, that is what before means. **Part Three, The Player,** is about you: making more money, getting around the right strangers, the posture that separates owners from office rats, the builder's chapter, and the goofball audit. **Part Four, The Endgame,** closes it: retirement, the estate, and the Game Plan, the ninety-day installation that converts this book from something you read into something that happened.

Every chapter runs the same spine, on purpose: the expensive lesson, the story and the scar, what nobody told you, the C.A.T. breakdown, the quarter lens, the move to make now, the warning, a checklist, and one closing club rule. The repetition is the design. I am not trying to entertain you twenty-three different ways. I am trying to install one operating system twenty-three times, from twenty-three directions, until it boots on its own.

Three requests before you start.

First, before you read Chapter 1, take three minutes and get your Before 40 Scorecard at before40club.com. It grades your Cash Flow, Assets, and Tax Planning today, before the book changes anything, and joining puts the weekly Brief and the club community behind you while you read. Every chapter lands harder when you know your own starting numbers, and the After version of that score, ninety days from now, is the whole point.

Second, do the moves. Every chapter ends with a Move to Make Now, and none of them are decorative. Most take under an hour. A reader who does the moves finishes this book with a running machine: the truth layer built, the reserve automated, the letters graded, the rooms booked, the professional hired, the ninety-day plan on the calendar. A reader who skips them finishes with a good memory. I have watched both readers for years, from across the desk, and I wrote this book for the first one.

Third, keep what I am about to say somewhere you can reach it on the hard days, because this book will occasionally read like an indictment of things you have already done. It is not. Chapter 1 says it and I will say it here first: nobody taught you, and that is not your fault. The wasted years, the container with nothing inside it, the house at the ceiling, the drawer with the envelope in it, all of it was the predictable output of playing an unexplained game, and every person in this club, including the one writing this sentence, has paid tuition to the same school. The fault question is boring and backward-facing. The only question this book cares about is forward-facing: now that somebody has finally told you, what happens next?

The quarters are running. Turn the page.

Welcome to the club.

PART I:

THE GAME

Six chapters, one job: the rulebook. The game you have been playing blind, the defaults you inherited, and the three letters that run everything after this page. Read Part I in order, because every exam and every play later in the book stands on this foundation.

CHAPTER 1:

NOBODY TAUGHT YOU THE MONEY GAME

"No one is coming to save you."

The Expensive Lesson

Here is the lesson this whole book is built on, and I am going to give it to you on page one because I am not in the business of making you wait for the point.

You have been playing a game your entire adult life that nobody taught you the rules to. The game has a scoreboard, referees, penalties, a clock, and a rulebook thousands of pages long. The other players, the ones who seem to keep winning, are not smarter than you. They read the rules, or they paid someone who did. You have been out there guessing.

And the tuition for guessing is brutal. It does not come as one big bill. It comes as a thousand quiet ones. The refund you celebrated that was actually your own money coming back to you with no interest. The LLC you formed because a video told you to, that changed nothing. The house you bought at the top of your approval instead of the top of your comfort. The IRS letter you ignored because you were scared of it, which is exactly how a small problem becomes a levy. The friend you funded. The partner you never had the money conversation with. Every one of those is tuition, paid to a school that never hands you a diploma.

I have spent 18 years across tax, accounting, startups, and real client money problems. I have read the tax returns of people who look rich and people who are actually free, and I can tell you they are usually not the same people. The difference between them is almost never income. It is whether anyone ever taught them the game.

Nobody taught you. That is not your fault.

Staying untaught after today is.

The Story

The moment the game became visible to me happened at KKR. I worked in the tax department during the day, and at night I rode the train to Fordham for my master's in taxation, so I was studying the rulebook in the evening and watching the varsity play at the highest level all day. And one day I watched a partner receive a million dollars in distributions. In one day.

Then I started reading how the wealthy actually score, because their returns spell it out. The W-2 income, the part taxed at the highest rates, might be two hundred fifty, three hundred, maybe half a million dollars. But then come the K-1s flowing off the partnerships, and that capital is riding long-term capital gains treatment. The structure was right there on paper: cash flow to fund the lifestyle, equity interests in the businesses doing the earning, and tax planning shielding the whole machine. They were not out-working anyone by ten times. They owned things, and they were structured. Even my own compensation was teaching the lesson, because part of it arrived as RSUs, my first personal taste of income that was not an hourly wage. That season, the day job and the night classes running in parallel, is where C.A.T. started crystallizing: how capital actually flows, how wealth is actually built, and how little of it my own neighborhood had ever been shown.

What that moment taught me is the thing I want tattooed on the inside of this book: the information was never hidden. It was just never handed to you. There is no vault. There is a rulebook, sitting in plain sight, that your school skipped, your parents may not have known, and your job has no incentive to explain. Your employer taught you exactly enough about money to cash your paycheck and contribute to the plan. That is not education. That is onboarding.

What Nobody Told You

Let me name the things you were supposed to figure out on your own.

Nobody told you that your salary is not your money

Your gross is a headline. Your take-home is the truth. Most people plan their lives off the headline and then wonder why the truth keeps embarrassing them every month. If you do not know your real monthly take-home number right now, without opening an app, you are playing the game blindfolded.

Nobody told you the tax code is a playbook, not a punishment

Most people experience taxes once a year, in April, as a verdict. But the code is not a verdict. It is a rulebook full of instructions that essentially say, if you do this, we will let you keep more. Own a business this way, keep this record, put money in this account, hold this asset this long. The people who win read it as instructions. The people who lose read it as a bill. April is too late. By April, the game is over and you are just finding out the score.

Nobody told you that your tax return is a scoreboard

Every year, that document tells you exactly how you played: how much came in, how much you kept, what you built, what you protected, what you gave away through pure inattention. Most people never read their own scoreboard. They sign where the preparer flags and file it in a drawer. Eighteen years of reading other people's scoreboards taught me that the return never lies. Show me three years of returns and I will tell you how someone thinks, what they fear, and whether they are building or just earning.

Nobody told you that income exposes your system. It does not fix it

This is the one that breaks people's hearts, so hear it early. If your money system is broken at $60,000, it is broken at $260,000. It is just broken with better scenery. I have sat with high earners who are one bad month from panic, and the problem was never the earning. More money poured into a broken system does not repair the system. It floods it.

Nobody told you there was a clock

Not a scary clock. A useful one. Your money life runs in quarters, like a game, and I will give you the full framework in a moment. But the short version is this: the moves that are cheap in one quarter are expensive in the next and sometimes impossible in the one after that. Compounding, entity structure, insurance, buying assets, teaching your kids: all of it is quarter-sensitive. Nobody handed you the game clock, so you have been playing like the game has no halves. It does.

Nobody told you that the big life events are the game's exam days

Marriage. The house. The kids. The business. The IRS letter. The inheritance. Each one looks like a life moment, and each one is secretly a money exam that grades you on preparation you were supposed to do months or years earlier. Marriage is love, and it is also a financial merger, with filing statuses, debts, and structures that merge whether you discussed them or not. The house is a dream, and it is also the largest tax and cash flow decision most people ever make, usually made in a weekend, on emotion, at the top of an approval number a bank picked. The letter from the IRS is scary, and it is also frequently wrong, which only helps the people who open it. Nobody told you the exams were coming, so you have been walking into them cold. This book is the study guide, and it is organized around exactly these events, because that is where the game actually gets won and lost. Not in apps. In moments.

And nobody told you the price of waiting, in actual numbers

The expensive way is not a metaphor. Waiting has a rate. A dollar put to work at 30 has decades more compounding than the same dollar at 45, and no amount of Q3 hustle buys those years back. An entity structured wrong at formation can quietly forfeit a tax-free exit that would have been worth more than every salary you ever earned. A W-4 left on autopilot leaks every paycheck for years. An ignored notice turns a disagreement into a levy. None of these require you to be foolish. They only require you to wait. Waiting is the tuition plan, and it enrolls you by default.

The C.A.T. Breakdown

Everything in this book runs through one method. Three letters. If you remember nothing else, remember these, because every chapter, every checklist, and every hard conversation ahead comes back to them.

C is Cash Flow. Know what actually comes in, control what goes out, and treat taxes as a monthly cash flow reality, not an annual ambush. Cash flow is the truth layer. Everything else is built on it, which is why people who skip it end up decorating a house with no foundation.

A is Assets. Stop renting out your hours as your only business model. Hours have a ceiling and your body sets it. Assets are things that earn when you are not in the room: a business with systems, equity, real estate, intellectual property. The people who got free did not simply out-earn everyone. They owned something.

T is Tax Planning. Structure everything so you keep more of what your cash flow and your assets produce. Planning, not filing. Filing is recording history. Planning is writing it. Your LLC did not save you taxes. Your structure might. The entity is a container, and what you do inside the container is the strategy.

Here is how the three work together, and why the order matters. Cash flow funds the assets. Assets multiply the cash flow. Tax planning protects both. Skip C and you have nothing to invest. Skip A and you work forever. Skip T and you build a beautiful machine with a leak in the bottom. The game is all three, run in a loop, for the rest of your life. That is the whole religion. Chapter 3 is the full sermon.

The Quarter Lens

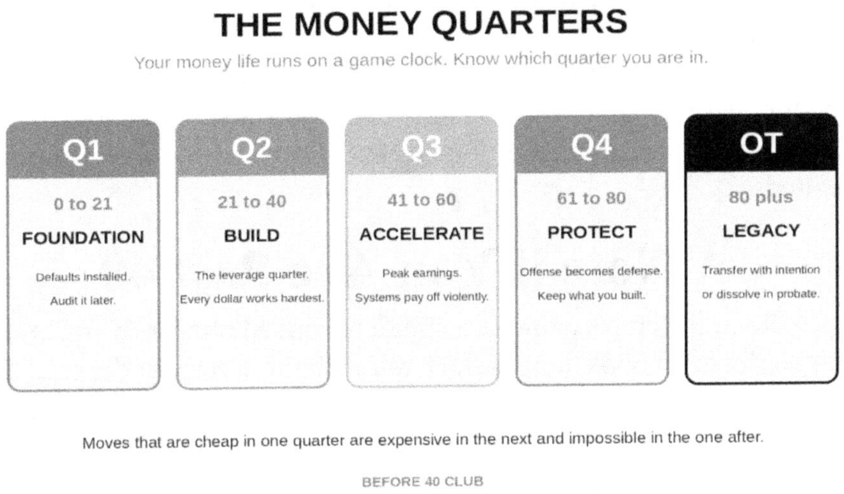

The Money Quarters: the five periods of your financial life

Your money life is a game with five periods, and knowing which one you are in changes what the right move is.

Q1, ages 0 to 21: Foundation. You did not control this quarter. Your habits, your money memories, and your defaults were installed here, mostly by people who were never taught the game either. You do not get to replay Q1. You do get to audit it, and Chapter 2 will make you.

Q2, ages 21 to 40: Build. This is the leverage quarter. Time is still massively on your side, mistakes are still recoverable, and every dollar you put to work here does more than it will ever do again. It is also the quarter people waste most completely, on looking successful instead of becoming free. If you are in Q2, this book is arriving on time.

Q3, ages 41 to 60: Accelerate. Peak earning years. The quarter where a system pays off violently and the absence of one becomes impossible to hide. Q3 with a system is a runway. Q3 without one is a treadmill with a countdown.

Q4, ages 61 to 80: Protect. The game shifts from offense to defense. Keeping, structuring, and not getting picked apart by taxes, health costs, and bad decisions made under pressure.

Overtime, 80 and beyond: Legacy. What you built either transfers with intention or dissolves in probate, family fights, and taxes nobody planned for. Overtime is decided decades earlier. It always is.

The Before 40 Club is not about your age. It is about the decision to stop learning money lessons the expensive way. Some join at 28. Some join at 52 wishing they joined at 28. Both are welcome. Only one waited.

A Note if You Are Past 40

Read the club's name as a standard, not a bouncer. If you are in Q3 holding this book, here is the truth without flattery or despair: the quarters compress, they do not close. The method is identical at 47 and at 27, the math simply asks for larger monthly numbers and fewer wasted months, and the code itself acknowledges you with catch-up provisions built for exactly this season. You also hold something no Q2 reader has: decades of pattern data about your own earning, spending, and industry, which Chapter 19 will teach you to treat as an asset. The best time to run this system was Q2. The second best time is the week you are in. Everything in this book applies to you, starting with the next chapter, minus only the excuse of time you cannot spend anyway.

The Move to Make Now

Do not finish this chapter and feel inspired. Feeling inspired is free and it produces nothing. Do this instead, this week.

Pull your last tax return. The full return, not the refund number. Sit with it for thirty minutes and answer three questions in writing. One: what was my real take-home after everything, divided by twelve. Two: what on this return earned money without my hours. Three: what did I do all year, on purpose, to lower this bill legally. For most people the honest answers are: I do not know, nothing, and nothing.

Good. Now you have a scoreboard and a starting line. You cannot fix a game you refuse to look at.

Let me tell you what to actually look at, because most people have never been taught to read their own return. Look at total income, then look at total tax, and divide. That is your effective rate, the real price you paid to play last year, and you should know it by heart the way you know your rent. Look at what kind of income it was: if every dollar came from a W-2, your entire financial life currently depends on one payer, one boss, and one set of hours, and that is not a judgment, it is a diagnosis. Look at your withholding against your tax: a big refund means you overpaid all year and financed the government for free; a big balance due means nobody was watching your year while it was still fixable. Look at the deductions and credits pages and ask a simple question: did I plan any of this, or did it just happen to me?

Thirty minutes. One document. Most people will learn more about their real financial life in that half hour than they learned in the previous decade. That is not because the exercise is genius. It is because they never looked.

The Warning

Here is what will actually happen for most people who read this chapter. They will nod. They will feel the little spark of, I need to get serious. And then the Office Rat version of them will take back over by Thursday: the low-agency 9 to 5 self that waits for permission, performs busyness, and calls a pay raise a plan. The Office Rat does not read tax returns. The Office Rat forwards memes about taxes and then overpays them.

Nobody is coming to teach you this. Not your job, not the government, not an app. Nobody cares more than you will. If you wait to be taught, you will be taught the expensive way, because the expensive way is the default. It is what happens automatically when you do nothing.

The Checklist

☐ Print or pull up your most recent full tax return

☐ Write down your real monthly take-home number from memory, then verify it

☐ Identify every line on your return that represents money earned without your hours (be honest if the answer is none)

☐ Write down the last deliberate tax planning move you made, and the date (be honest if the answer is never)

☐ Identify your current Money Quarter and say it out loud

The Before 40 Club Rule

The game does not care whether you know the rules. Learn them anyway, because the tuition for guessing never stops billing.

One question before you go. What lesson have I already paid full tuition on, and what did it cost?

Put this chapter to work in the companion Before 40 Club Workbook at before40club.com.

CHAPTER 2:

THE Q1 AUDIT: WHERE YOUR MONEY DEFAULTS CAME FROM

"Wealth creation is an evolution of yourself."

The Expensive Lesson

You did not choose your money habits. You inherited them, the way you inherited your accent.

Before you ever earned a dollar, you were running someone else's money operating system. It got installed between the ages of 0 and 21, in Q1, the quarter you did not control, by people who were mostly never taught the game either. The way your household talked about money, or refused to. Whether bills were a rhythm or an emergency. Whether the arrival of money meant relief, celebration, secrecy, or conflict. Whether anyone in the house owned anything, or everyone worked for someone who did. All of it went in early, silently, and it has been making your financial decisions ever since while you took the credit and the blame.

Here is why this chapter comes before the strategies. Every technique in this book gets executed by the person Q1 built. Hand a perfect system to someone running a broken default and the default wins, quietly, within months. I have watched clients nod through a flawless plan and then violate it by the next quarter, not because they were weak, but because nobody ever showed them the software they were running. You cannot override code you have never read.

The expensive lesson is this: most of what you call your personality with money is actually your programming with money, and programming can be audited. People pay for decades because they treat their defaults as identity. This chapter is where you stop doing that.

The Story

I grew up in Nigeria, and the money atmosphere of my childhood had a signature: my father owned things. He ran a veterinary medicine business. He ran his own fumigation business. Whatever the season asked of him, my dad built something of his own to answer it, and my mother and father together made sure we were provided for and pushed toward a better life than the one they started with. So the default that got installed in me, before I could name it, was that ownership was normal. Working for yourself was not a risk somebody in our house took once. It was simply what my father did, the way other fathers had employers.

That default followed me across an ocean and into every room I have ever worked in. Through the accounting firms, through private equity, through the controller years, some quiet part of me was always measuring the distance back to what my father modeled, and the day I finally started my own firm, I was not becoming something new. I was returning to the family setting. He passed away on December 8, and this book carries his name in the front of it, because the most valuable thing in it, the belief that you can own your own life, was his before it was mine.

Here is the scene I carry. The front of our house was the storefront, my father's veterinary business, and the back of the house was where we lived, so the family home and the family business shared one roof and one door. I remember him waking up early and diligently, on the phone with his CPAs, making sure the books were in order. I remember him coordinating with his attorneys and his accountants like a man running an institution, because to him it was one. I remember animals coming home with him to be nurtured and cared for, and I remember the hospitality, the way he treated every customer like they were the whole business, because they were. Before I ever heard the word entrepreneur, I had watched one make his coffee every morning.

I share that not for sympathy but for method. Nothing in my Q1 was my fault, and everything it installed became my responsibility the day I noticed it. That sentence is the entire chapter. Read it again.

What Nobody Told You

Nobody told you that money scripts are real and yours are running right now

A money script is a belief installed early that executes automatically. Money is scarce and disappears. Money is what good people do not talk about. Money means someone is about to argue. Rich people did something wrong to get there. We do not ask for help. We take care of everybody. There is always more where that came from. You can hear your own scripts if you listen for the sentences that come out of your mouth about money without any thinking attached. Those sentences were written decades ago, usually by someone else.

Nobody told you that your parents were improvising

This one sets people free. The adults who raised you were not withholding the money game from you. In most houses, they did not have it to give. They passed down what they had: work ethic, sacrifice, survival skills, sometimes fear, sometimes silence. You can honor everything they gave you and still refuse to inherit their ceilings. Gratitude and upgrade are not opposites. The Before 40 Club is full of people who are the first in their family to read the rulebook, and being first is heavier and better than being handed it.

Nobody told you that your first paycheck was a fork in the road

Somewhere in late Q1 or early Q2, money started arriving with your name on it, and in that moment your defaults took the wheel for the first time with real fuel. Whatever you did with your first real checks, spent to feel it, saved out of fear, sent it home, performed with it, is a nearly perfect snapshot of your installation. Not your character. Your installation. Most people have never once examined that snapshot.

Nobody told you that environment outranks intention

Q1 also installed your normal: what a normal car is, a normal vacation, a normal amount of debt, a normal way to handle a windfall. Normal is the most expensive word in your vocabulary, because you will drift toward it under pressure no matter what you intend. The audit is not just about beliefs. It is about recalibrating what normal means before Q2 and Q3 spend the difference.

And nobody told you that the audit is the upgrade

You do not fix defaults by hating them. You fix them by naming them. A default, once named, becomes a decision. Unnamed, it stays destiny. That is why this chapter has homework and the homework is writing. Vague awareness changes nothing. Paper changes people.

The C.A.T. Breakdown

Run the audit through the letters, because your Q1 installed a default setting for each one.

C, your cash flow default. What did money arriving mean in your house, and what did money leaving mean? Households teach one of a few C defaults: money is managed (rare), money is survived (common), money is performed (expensive), or money is ignored until it screams (the most expensive). Your adult relationship with checking your accounts, opening mail, and knowing your numbers is downstream of this. If looking at your money makes your chest tight, that is not laziness. That is an installed alarm, and it can be uninstalled through repetition: small, scheduled, boring looks until looking is neutral.

A, your assets default. Here is the sharpest question in the chapter: did anyone in your Q1 own anything that earned without their hours? A business, property, equity, anything? For most people the honest answer is no, and that means your installation has no template for ownership. Employment is the only model in your source code. That explains why building an asset feels unnatural and renting out hours feels safe, even when the math says the opposite. You are not bad at ownership. You are unexposed to it. Exposure is fixable, and Chapter 17 (GAS) is the fix.

T, your tax default. What did your house believe about the IRS and the system? Fear, avoidance, resentment, or literacy? Most Q1 installations file taxes the way they pay parking tickets: an annual annoyance handled at the last minute with a flinch. Almost no household models taxes as a planning discipline, which is why April is too late is news to grown adults with six-figure incomes. Your tax default is probably avoidance with a side of fear. Name it, and Chapter 6 replaces it.

The Quarter Lens

Q1 (0 to 21): You are reading this chapter about it, or you are a parent currently writing someone else's Q1. If it is the second one, understand the stakes: your kids are not learning your money speeches. They are learning your money atmosphere. The account you open for them matters less than the calm or panic they absorb when money gets discussed. Chapter 9 goes deep, but plant the flag here: the cheapest wealth transfer in existence is a well-installed Q1, and it costs behavior, not dollars.

Q2 (21 to 40): The audit quarter. This is when defaults do maximum damage because income finally gives them fuel, and it is also when overwriting them is cheapest, because habits are younger and stakes are smaller. Every year the audit gets delayed, the defaults compound alongside your salary.

Q3 (41 to 60): Unaudited defaults at Q3 income are a wrecking ball. This is where the performed-money default buys the overextended house and the survival default hoards cash out of fear while inflation eats it. The audit still works in Q3. It just has more cleanup attached.

Q4 and Overtime: The defaults you never audited become the ones you hand down. Unexamined Q1 programming is the only inheritance that transfers with one hundred percent certainty and zero paperwork.

The Move to Make Now

Write your money autobiography. One sitting, sixty minutes, by hand or typed, nobody ever has to see it.

Answer these, in order, with scenes and not summaries. What is my earliest money memory? What did money arriving mean in my house? What did money leaving mean? What did my family own that earned without hours? What sentences about money did I hear repeated? What did I do with my first real paycheck, and why? What money behavior do I have today that I can now trace straight back?

Then finish with the two lists that convert this from therapy to strategy. List one: three defaults I am keeping, on purpose, because they serve me. List two: three defaults I am overwriting, named specifically, with the replacement behavior written next to each. Not I will be better with money. Instead: default, avoids looking at accounts; replacement, ten-minute money review every Sunday at 9am, calendar recurring.

Named, scheduled, done. That is how software gets patched.

The Warning

Two ditches on either side of this chapter, and people crash into both.

Ditch one is blame. The audit is not a trial of your parents. The moment this becomes a story about what they did to you, you have traded a tool for an excuse, and excuses pay nothing. Purpose comes first, and the purpose here is your next forty years, not your last twenty. Honor the people, audit the programming, move.

Ditch two is exemption. Some of you grew up comfortable, maybe even around money, and you are tempted to skip this chapter. Do not. Comfortable Q1s install their own defaults: safety nets that muted urgency, normals calibrated to someone else's balance sheet, an allergy to the boring work because things always worked out. Nobody is bigger than the program, and the audit finds everyone.

The Checklist

☐ Write the money autobiography in one 60-minute sitting, scenes not summaries

☐ Identify your household's C default, A default, and T default in one sentence each

☐ Write down your first-paycheck snapshot honestly

☐ List three inherited defaults you are keeping on purpose

☐ List three defaults you are overwriting, each with a named, scheduled replacement behavior

The Before 40 Club Rule

Your defaults were installed without your permission. They only keep running with it.

One question before you go. Which inherited default is still running my money today?

Put this chapter to work in the companion Before 40 Club Workbook at before40club.com.

CHAPTER 3:

THE C.A.T. METHOD

"Cash flow gives you options. Assets create freedom. Tax planning helps you keep it."

The Expensive Lesson

Every expensive money mistake I have witnessed in 18 years, and I have witnessed thousands, collapses into a failure of one of three things. The person did not control their cash flow, so there was never anything to build with. Or they never bought assets, so they rented out their hours until their hours ran out. Or they never planned their taxes, so they built something real and then handed a huge slice of it back through pure inattention.

That is it. That is the entire taxonomy of financial pain. The guy who makes $400,000 and feels broke: cash flow failure. The woman who worked 30 loyal years and has a pension and a prayer: assets failure. The founder who sold his company and lost millions of the exit to a structure he set up wrong on day one: tax planning failure. Different faces, different incomes, same three doors.

So I stopped giving people fifty rules. Fifty rules is how you guarantee somebody follows none of them. I give them three letters instead.

C.A.T. Cash Flow. Assets. Tax Planning.

Master your cash flow, buy the right assets, and plan your taxes around both. That is the whole game. Everything else in personal finance is commentary.

The Story

The method came from the returns. Thousands of them, across a professional career, plus the audit of my own life, which is the return you read the hardest. And somewhere in a stretch of client meetings it snapped into focus: everybody had the same diagnosis. The entry points were different, the incomes were different, the industries were different, but the failure was always one of three doors, and the doors had an order. You cannot have the A without the C, because assets are bought with cash flow. You cannot have the C and the A without the T, because unprotected machines leak. The first thing I tell every client is the same thing regardless of their zeros: model the cash flow first, because you can tell me you make whatever you make, but what is the true after-tax number? Everything starts there.

The back half of my client book today is multimillionaires, including clients who have exited into seven, eight, and nine figure outcomes, and here is what those files teach about the A: you have twenty-four hours in a day and you need eight of them to sleep. If you have a family, the math gets tighter. So the asset column gets built one of two ways, by focusing ruthlessly on your strengths, or by building a team and a network that builds it with you. Either way, the letters are not a theory I invented. They are a pattern I surrendered to, one return at a time.

The reason I teach it as an acronym is not cuteness. It is retention under pressure. When you are standing in a dealership, or reading a scary letter, or listening to a friend pitch you an opportunity, you will not remember a chapter. You will remember three letters. C.A.T. is designed to be the thing that shows up in the room with you when I am not there.

What Nobody Told You

Nobody told you that these three are a system, not a menu. People treat personal finance like a buffet. They pick the plate they like. Some people love budgeting, so they do C forever and wonder why frugality never made anyone free. Some people love the idea of assets, so they buy a rental with no reserves and get taught the C lesson by a broken boiler in February. Some people fetishize tax tricks they saw online, T with no C and no A, which is how you end up with an S-Corp election on a business that makes $30,000 and now has payroll costs it cannot carry.

The letters are in order for a reason. C funds A. A multiplies C. T protects both. You do not get to skip a letter. You only get to choose whether you learn that now or expensively.

C: Cash Flow

Cash flow is the truth layer, and most people are running from the truth.

Your cash flow is three numbers. What actually comes in each month, after taxes, for real. What actually goes out, for real, including the spending you pretend is an exception every single month. And the gap. That gap is your entire financial future in one number. A positive gap, deployed on purpose, becomes assets. A negative gap, ignored, becomes debt, panic, and eventually the kind of decisions people make when they are cornered.

Here is the part that makes me the annoying uncle at the table: taxes live inside C, not in April. If you are self-employed or own a business and money comes in without a tax reserve coming out, you are not keeping that money. You are holding it for the IRS and calling it yours. Every dollar in, a percentage moves to a separate reserve account before you touch a cent. That account is not yours. You are the custodian. Do this one thing and you will never be blindsided in April again, and you will be ahead of the majority of business owners I have ever met.

And hear this clearly, because it is the C-side sermon: income exposes your system. It does not fix it. Raises do not fix leaks. They pressurize them.

One more C truth. You cannot save your way to free. Cash flow control is necessary and insufficient. At some point the answer is MMM: Make More Money. Earn more, and run the additional money through a system instead of a lifestyle. The system is what turns MMM into freedom instead of just louder brokeness.

A: Assets

An asset, in this book, means one thing: something that earns without your hours.

That definition matters because the world keeps handing you fake ones. The car is not an asset. The watch is not an asset. Even the house you live in is mostly a liability wearing an asset costume; it takes money every month and pays you in shelter and hope. Real assets, the kind this letter is about, put money in your account while you sleep, travel, or sit in a hospital bed. A business with systems that run without you. Equity in something growing. Real estate that cash flows. A book, a product, a piece of intellectual property that sells while you do something else.

Why does A matter so much? Because your default business model, the one you were handed, is renting out your hours. Hours are the worst inventory on earth. You cannot manufacture more, you cannot store them, and your only pricing strategies are work more of them or charge more for each one. Both have ceilings and one of them is your health. I have read the returns. The people who got free were not simply the highest earners. Plenty of high earners are one bad month from panic. The free ones owned something that paid them when they were not working. That is the entire distinction between looking rich and being free.

Your first asset does not need to be impressive. It needs to exist. The gap between zero assets and one small asset is a different life. The gap between one asset and five is just math.

And a warning that belongs under A: Get Around Strangers. GAS. Your current circle mostly knows what you know and owns what you own. Assets, deals, and opportunities travel through rooms, and most of the rooms that will change your life are currently full of strangers. The Office Rat stays with the familiar and calls it loyalty. The builder goes and gets around strangers on purpose.

T: Tax Planning

Tax planning is the difference between filing and planning, and almost everyone you know only files.

Filing is recording history. It happens after the year is over, when every option is already dead. Planning is writing history. It happens during the year, while the moves are still available. The entity election, the retirement contribution, the timing of income, the paying of your kids legally through the business, the hold period on the stock, the reserve, the records. All of it is a during-the-year sport. April is too late. April is the autopsy.

Let me kill the most expensive myth in this letter while we are here. Your LLC did not save you taxes. Your structure might. A basic LLC is taxed exactly like you with no LLC. It is a legal container, and containers do not create savings. What moves the number is what you run inside the container: the right election at the right income level, a reasonable salary done correctly, clean books, a reserve, a rhythm of estimated payments, and a planner who looks at your year before it ends instead of after. Most people stop at the container and wonder why nothing changed.

T is also the letter of respect. Not fear, respect. You do not cheat, you do not play in gray areas some guy on the internet promised were loopholes, and you do not ignore letters. You learn the rules and you use every single one of them that was written for you. The code is full of instructions that reward owners, builders, savers, and planners. Take the rewards. Leave the fantasies.

The C.A.T. Breakdown

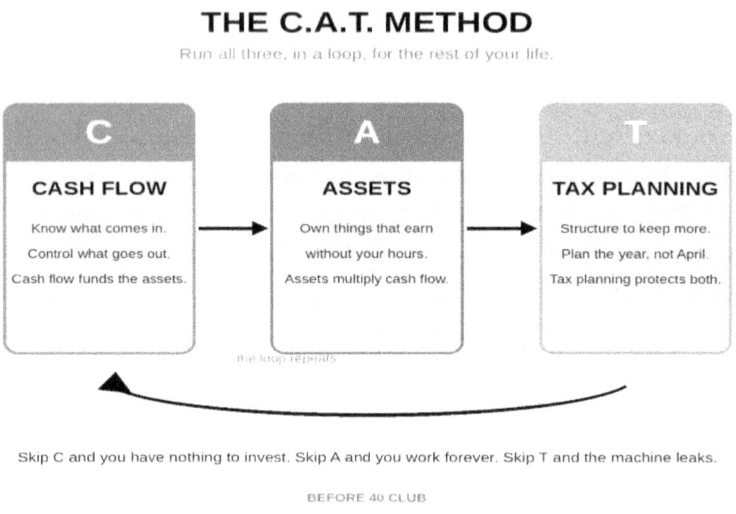

The C.A.T. Method: Cash Flow funds Assets, Assets multiply Cash Flow, Tax Planning protects both

This chapter is the method, so let me show you the loop running, because C.A.T. is not three chores. It is one engine.

Cash flow discipline creates a monthly surplus. The surplus, deployed on purpose instead of absorbed by lifestyle, buys assets. The assets produce new income that does not cost hours, which widens the surplus. Tax planning wraps around the whole loop so that at every stage, income arriving, assets bought, assets sold, business run, you keep the maximum the rules allow. Then the bigger, protected surplus buys better assets, and the loop turns again.

Run that loop for ten years and you are unrecognizable. Skip one letter and the loop stalls exactly there. No C: nothing to deploy. No A: a hamster wheel with good credit. No T: a leak that scales with your success, which is the cruelest kind, because the better you do, the more you lose.

When you face any money decision from now on, and I mean any, run the letters. Does this improve or damage my cash flow? Is this an asset or a costume? What is the tax move before, not after? Three questions, ten seconds, and you will already be operating above almost everyone in your life.

Let me show you the letters running on real decisions, the exact ones this book keeps returning to, so you can hear the method in the wild.

The house. The bank hands you an approval number and everyone treats it like a recommendation. Run the letters instead. C: the mortgage is not the cost; the cost is the mortgage plus property taxes plus insurance plus maintenance plus reserves, tested against your real take-home, and stress-tested against three bad months. The bank tells you the max. C.A.T. tells you the right number. A: a primary home is shelter first and an asset costume second, so do not drain every reserve dollar into the down payment of a costume. T: understand before you offer, not after, how this purchase changes next April, and if you are self-employed, know that the aggressive write-offs that saved you tax are the same lines that can sink your approval. Same document, two different games, and you needed to know that two years ago.

The marriage. Everyone plans the wedding. Run the letters on the merger. C: two incomes, two spending systems, one household, and the honest conversation about what actually comes in and goes out for each of you. A: what does each person own, owe, and build, and what happens to the building when it is joint? T: filing jointly or separately is a real decision with real numbers, one person's old tax debt can become a shared problem, and a spouse who owns a business changes everything about the return. Marriage is love. It is also a filing status.

The LLC. Run the letters on the thing the internet told you to form. C: does the business have a reserve, a payment rhythm, and books, or just a name and a logo? A: is this an asset that could ever run without your hours, or is it your job wearing a container? T: the container saved you nothing; the election, the salary, the records, and the plan are where the number moves. Three questions and you just skipped five years of expensive confusion.

That is the method. Not a philosophy. A reflex. The chapters ahead just keep installing it, event by event, until it fires on its own.

The Quarter Lens

The method is the same in every quarter. The weighting is not.

Q1 (0 to 21): C.A.T. is installed here as habit, mostly by watching. If you are a parent, understand that your kids are learning your real method, not your speeches.

Q2 (21 to 40): Heavy C, aggressive A, foundational T. This is the quarter to build the cash flow system, buy your first assets while time is still your partner, and get the structure right so your Q3 is not spent repairing your Q2. Every big Q2 move, the marriage, the house, the business, is a C.A.T. exam in disguise.

Q3 (41 to 60): Peak earnings meet the loop at full speed. A compounds, T gets sophisticated, and the gap between the people who ran the method in Q2 and the people who did not becomes visible from space.

Q4 (61 to 80): T moves to the front. Protection, distribution order, keeping what the loop built from being carved up.

Overtime (80+): The method's final exam is whether it transfers. Legacy is C.A.T. taught, structured, and handed off on purpose.

One more claim before the health application, and I make it with eighteen years of evidence: the method is universal. It does not care whether you earn a salary or own the building, whether you drive a truck or run a fund, whether your number has four digits or nine. Every financial life on earth has money coming in, things that could be owned, and a tax authority with opinions, which means every financial life on earth runs on C, A, and T whether its owner knows it or not. The method scales from a first paycheck to a nine-figure exit without changing a letter, it works in every state and most countries, and it works at every table size: run it alone, run it as a couple, run it as a household, and start the children as young as five, Chapter 9 shows you how, because a family that shares one operating system stops having money fights and starts having money meetings.

Health Through C.A.T.

One more application before the moves, planted here on purpose so you carry it through every chapter that follows: the method runs on your body, and the method also runs your body. C: health is a cash flow category, not an afterthought, the insurance premium, the real food, the preventive care, the gym, the therapy or coaching when it is needed, all of it planned and funded like any other non-negotiable line. A: your body, your energy, your attention, and your clarity are the assets underneath every other asset you will ever build, the machine that produces everything the rest of this book describes, which makes your body the first business you are responsible for operating. T: the code itself rewards planning here, the HSA from Chapter 21, the FSA, the disability protection, the employer benefits most people never read, all reviewed before a health crisis instead of during one. Chapter 23 hands you my whole protocol. For now, just carry the frame: every letter has a health application, and skipping them costs compound interest too.

The Move to Make Now

Grade yourself tonight. One letter grade for each letter, and no grade inflation, because nobody is watching and lying to yourself is the most expensive habit in this book.

C: Do I know my real monthly numbers and does a tax reserve come off the top automatically? A: Do I own anything at all that earns without my hours? T: Did I make one deliberate, legal tax planning move in the last twelve months, during the year, on purpose?

Write the three grades somewhere you will see them. Your lowest grade is your assignment, and the chapters ahead are organized to raise it. Do not work on your favorite letter. Work on your worst one. The loop stalls at the weakest letter every time.

The Warning

The danger of a simple framework is that simple sounds easy, and you will be tempted to nod at C.A.T. instead of running it. Knowing the letters is worth nothing. I know overweight doctors and broke accountants. The method only pays the people who run it monthly, in order, on their worst letter first, for years.

And no one is bigger than the program. Not the high earner who thinks income exempts him from C. Not the hustler who thinks vibes exempt him from T. Not me. The moment you decide you are special is the moment the expensive school reopens enrollment, and it always has a seat for you.

The Checklist

☐ Write your three real cash flow numbers: in, out, gap

☐ Open a separate tax reserve account and set an automatic percentage transfer

☐ List every true asset you own (earns without your hours) - a short honest list beats a long flattering one

☐ Write down your entity and structure, and the date anyone last reviewed it

☐ Grade yourself C, A, and T, and circle the lowest grade

The Before 40 Club Rule

Cash flow funds the assets. Assets multiply the cash flow. Tax planning protects both. Run the loop or the loop runs you.

One question before you go. Which letter, C, A, or T, is weakest in my life right now?

Put this chapter to work in the companion Before 40 Club Workbook at before40club.com.

CHAPTER 4:

CASH FLOW: THE TRUTH LAYER

"Small financial decisions compound with every paycheck."

The Expensive Lesson

Most people do not have an income problem. They have a truth problem.

Ask someone what they make and they will quote you their salary, a gross annual number that no one has ever actually received. Ask them what they spend and they will quote you a fantasy, a budget that exists in an app and dies every month around the 19th. Between those two fictions is where financial lives quietly fall apart, at every income level, and I mean every. I have sat across from people earning $500,000 whose cash flow, once we told the truth about it, looked like a person earning $80,000 with better restaurants.

Cash flow is the truth layer of your entire financial life. It is three numbers: what actually comes in each month after taxes, what actually goes out including all the exceptions you pretend are exceptions, and the gap between them. That gap is your future. A positive gap, deployed on purpose, becomes assets, options, and calm. A negative or zero gap becomes debt, panic, and a life spent one surprise away from crisis, regardless of how impressive the gross number is.

The expensive lesson: you cannot build anything on numbers you refuse to know. Every strategy in this book, every asset in Chapter 5, every tax move in Chapter 6, is funded by the gap. No gap, no game. This chapter is where we go find yours.

The Story

Let me tell you about a client whose feed you would have envied. High income, the Rolexes, the house, the travel. Here is the thing about social media: you see what they post. You do not see what they file with the IRS. I see it. I know what they actually do.

This client netted about one and a half million dollars in a year. When we built the truth layer together, real deposits, real outflows, the amount that actually stayed was about one hundred fifty thousand, and the lifestyle was calibrated like the income was two million. High earners are the least likely people to budget, especially the self-employed, who spend against gross cash flow as if the IRS were not a silent partner in every deposit. So I put the numbers in front of him and said it plainly: your cash burn cannot currently support any tax planning at all, because there is nothing stable enough to plan around. There is no budget in this life. And some of this spending is not for you, it is for outside validation. I review my own bank statements monthly, sometimes weekly, just to see what changed, and I told him that too, because the discipline I was asking of him is one I practice. What changed in his face in that meeting is what changes in everyone's: the income had been so loud for so long that he had never once heard the numbers.

The pattern behind that story repeats weekly in my office: income exposes your system. It does not fix it. The raise, the bonus, the big year, they pour more water into whatever bucket you have. If the bucket leaks, more water just means a bigger puddle. Fix the bucket first. The bucket is this chapter.

What Nobody Told You

Nobody told you what your paycheck actually is

Your paycheck is a settlement between you, the government, and your own past decisions, and most people have never audited the settlement. Gross pay at the top is the fiction. Then federal withholding, which is not your tax bill, it is a guess at your tax bill, controlled by a form you filled out on your first day and never touched again. Then state, then FICA, then benefits, then the retirement contribution. What lands is your real number, and your real number divided into your real month is the only income figure that means anything. If you cannot say your monthly take-home out loud right now, you have been planning your life with a number you do not know.

Nobody told you the W-4 is a steering wheel, not a formality

That form controls the guess. Set it wrong in one direction and you owe in April with penalties waving. Set it wrong in the other direction and you get the thing people brag about: the refund. Let me say this the way I say it in the office. A big refund is not a win. It means you overpaid all year, gave the government an interest-free loan, and threw a party when they returned your own money. That money belonged in your paycheck every two weeks, paying down the card charging you 24 percent, or feeding the gap. The goal is not a big refund. The goal is owing nothing and being owed nothing. The W-4 needs a review after every life change: marriage, house, kid, side income, second job, raise. Two incomes with unadjusted withholding is one of the most common surprise tax bills in America, and it is a ten-minute fix.

Nobody told you that the out number lies more than the in number

People know roughly what they make. Almost nobody knows what they spend, because spending hides in three costumes. The subscriptions costume: small recurring charges that individually feel like nothing and collectively fund someone else's asset. The exceptions costume: the wedding, the repair, the trip, the annual insurance, each one treated as a one-time event even though some exception arrives every single month, which makes exceptions a category, not an event. And the identity costume: the spending you do not examine because examining it threatens who you think you are. The truth layer requires ninety days of real data, every dollar, no editing. Not to judge it. To see it. You cannot steer what you will not look at.

Nobody told you the gap has a job

The gap is not savings in the vague sense. The gap has assignments, in order. First assignment: the tax reserve, if any of your income arrives without withholding. Self-employed, business owner, side income, bonus-heavy: a fixed percentage of every dollar in moves to a separate account before you touch a cent. That account is not yours. You are the custodian, and April stops being an ambush forever. Second assignment: the emergency reserve, boring, liquid, months of real expenses, sized to your volatility. Third assignment: assets, which is Chapter 5, and the reason the first two exist. A gap with no assignments evaporates. It always evaporates. Money without orders goes AWOL.

And nobody told you that automation beats character

You will not out-discipline a broken flow, because discipline is a battery and life drains it. The people whose cash flow works did not become monks. They built plumbing. Money arrives and splits automatically: reserve percentage here, fixed costs account there, investing pulled before it is ever visible, spending money in its own container with a hard edge. Automate savings before you see the money, because the version of you that sees the money cannot be trusted, and that is not an insult, that is every human ever tested. Set the pipes so the right thing happens when you are tired, distracted, and celebrating. That is the whole trick.

The C.A.T. Breakdown

C: This entire chapter is C, but here is C in one sentence: know the three numbers, widen the gap from both ends, and give every gap dollar a written assignment. Widening from both ends matters. Cutting alone has a floor, you can only cut to zero, and living at the floor makes people quit the whole program. Earning has no ceiling, which is why MMM, Make More Money, is a cash flow strategy and not just ambition. But new money enters the same pipes, so build the pipes first or MMM just buys a bigger puddle.

A: The gap is the factory that produces assets. Every recurring cost you carry is anti-asset: it is you funding someone else's cash flow with yours. Before any purchase that adds a monthly payment, run the question: whose asset is this payment building? Sometimes the answer is acceptably yours, a mortgage on the right house, a loan on a machine that earns. Usually the answer is theirs. Count your monthly payments tonight and sort them into building mine versus building theirs. That sort will bother you. Good.

T: Taxes are the largest single line in your cash flow and the only one people review annually instead of monthly. Bring T into the month: the reserve percentage on untaxed income, the W-4 tuned to reality, estimated payments on a calendar rhythm instead of a panic, and the effective rate you know by heart. Treating taxes as cash flow planning instead of a once-a-year event is the single most CPA sentence in this book, and it will save you more stress than any deduction ever found in April.

The Quarter Lens

Q1: The atmosphere chapter already covered it, but note: children absorb cash flow rhythm before they can count. Calm, scheduled money handling is a curriculum.

Q2: Build the truth layer now, while the numbers are small and the habits are cheap. A Q2 that installs the three numbers, the reserve, and the automation graduates into Q3 with a machine. This is also the quarter where lifestyle wants to grow exactly as fast as income; the discipline is letting the gap capture the raises. Half of every raise to the gap, forever, is a rule that quietly makes people wealthy while their coworkers upgrade cars.

Q3: Peak income meets the truth layer, and the results split violently. With the machine: maximum accumulation years, assets stacking, tax planning with real ammunition. Without it: the highest-earning, brokest-feeling years of a person's life, plus the dawning math about time.

Q4: Cash flow inverts. The question becomes drawdown order, which is a tax question wearing a cash flow costume, and it is decided well by people who spent decades knowing their numbers and badly by people meeting them for the first time at 62.

Overtime: The truth layer becomes the estate's truth layer. Executors inherit your organization or your chaos. Chapter 13 carries this.

The Debt Layer: Cash Flow's Shadow

One more layer before the moves, because debt is cash flow's shadow: every balance you carry is a claim on future months, priced by a number most people have never treated as a price. Your credit score is not a grade on your character. It is the interest rate your life gets charged, on the mortgage, the car, the business line, sometimes even the insurance, which means a mediocre score is a permanent surcharge on everything and an excellent one is a discount you earn once and collect forever. Pay every account on time, keep card balances low against their limits, stop opening things you do not need, and the score maintains itself, quietly, like every other system in this book.

Then sort your debt honestly, because debt comes in two species wearing the same costume. Debt that buys assets, the mortgage on a cash-flowing property, the sensibly structured business loan, is leverage: it can accelerate the A in C.A.T. when the underlying math survives Chapter 14's spreadsheet. Debt that bought lifestyle, the card balances, the financed furniture, the car beyond the ratio, is a lien on your gap, compounding against you at rates no investment reliably beats. The paydown discipline is unglamorous: list every balance with its rate, aim the surplus at the most expensive one while paying minimums on the rest, and if your psychology needs early wins, kill the smallest balance first, because the method that gets finished beats the method that was optimal. What is never acceptable is the minimum-payment cruise, which is a subscription to staying exactly where you are. And student loans get named here because Chapter 21 will show you where they end up when ignored: in your fifties and sixties, still deducting from a retirement you needed whole. Price them, schedule them, and never cosign new ones against your own Q3.

The Move to Make Now

Three actions, this week, in order.

One: find your real take-home. Last paystub or last three months of deposits, converted to one monthly number, said out loud, written where you plan.

Two: pull the last 90 days of every account and card, and total the real out. No editing, no that was a one-time thing. Subtract. Meet your gap. Whatever it is, it is the truest financial fact you own.

Three: open the reserve account if any untaxed income touches you, set the automatic percentage, and set one automatic transfer to savings or investing dated the day after payday. Pipes before promises.

Then check your W-4 against your actual last-year tax outcome. Big refund or big bill, either way, adjust it. Ten minutes. Do not leave your paycheck on autopilot set by a form you signed years ago on your first day, standing at a counter, thinking about lunch.

The Warning

The failure mode of this chapter is not ignorance anymore. You now know. The failure mode is the Office Rat move: converting knowledge into a feeling of progress instead of pipes. Downloading the app is not the truth layer. Talking about the budget is not the truth layer. The Office Rat performs financial responsibility the way he performs work, visibly and without results. The builder installs plumbing once and lets it run.

And a warning for the strong earners specifically: you will be tempted to believe your income exempts you from the small numbers. It does not. I have read your returns for 18 years. The big incomes with no truth layer end up in my office with the same puddle as everyone else, just wearing better shoes. No one is bigger than the program.

The Checklist

☐ List every debt with its rate, sort asset debt from lifestyle debt, and aim the surplus at the most expensive lifestyle balance

☐ Write your real monthly take-home, verified against actual deposits

☐ Complete the 90-day spending truth pull, unedited

☐ Calculate and write down your gap

☐ Open a separate tax reserve account and automate the percentage (if any income arrives untaxed)

The Before 40 Club Rule

Your gap is your future arriving in monthly installments. Know it, widen it, and give every dollar of it a written job.

One question before you go. Where does my gap go each month without a written job?

Agency: Which of your three numbers is fully under your control today? **Urgency:** Which automated transfer goes live this week, dated the day after payday?

Put this chapter to work in the companion Before 40 Club Workbook at before40club.com.

CHAPTER 5:

ASSETS: STOP RENTING OUT YOUR HOURS

"People are trained to earn. Very few are taught to own."

The Expensive Lesson

Your default business model, the one you were handed without a conversation, is renting out your hours. One customer, called an employer. One product, called your time. One pricing meeting a year, called a review, where the customer decides what your product is worth and you say thank you.

Hours are the worst inventory on earth. You cannot manufacture more of them. You cannot store the unsold ones. Your total lifetime supply is unknown but fixed, and the quality of the remaining stock declines. There are exactly two ways to grow a business built on hours: sell more of them, which costs your health and your family, or charge more per hour, which has a ceiling set by your industry and your negotiating stomach. Every person you know who is exhausted and stuck is running this model at capacity and wondering why the math never changes.

The math never changes because the model cannot change. Only the model can change.

The expensive lesson of this chapter is the pattern I have watched for 18 years across every tax return I have ever read: the people who got free were not the highest earners. Plenty of high earners are one bad month from panic, because a high hourly rate is still an hourly life. The people who got free owned something that earned without their hours. That is the entire distinction between looking rich and being free, and by the end of this chapter you will never unsee it.

The Story

Two clients, close in age, tell this whole chapter. One was thirty-four, the other thirty-six, and their incomes were drastically different, with the second one earning far less. But when I put the two returns side by side, the lower earner was the free one. On her 1040, the story was on Schedule E: rental income, capital assets, money arriving whether or not she showed up anywhere. On his, the story was an impressive number built entirely out of hours, and hours have a ceiling with his name on it. Same decade of life, two completely different relationships with time.

My own first non-hourly dollar came during the pandemic. Small businesses were drowning in confusion about EIDL and the COVID relief loans, so I built a presentation, turned what I knew into tax planning courses, and sold them online. The first time money arrived from a course while I was doing something else entirely, the lesson landed in my body and not just my head: you do not have to trade your time for dollars. You trade your value. Package the value once and it can pay you a thousand times, which is the entire difference between the two returns at the top of this story.

After enough years, I stopped reading returns as tax documents and started reading them as biographies. A return tells you how someone's money arrives, and how money arrives tells you how someone lives. W-2 only: their time is owned. Business income with systems: their time is leveraged. Rental income, dividends, royalties, K-1s: their money works night shifts. Same city, same age, completely different lives, and the difference was never intelligence. It was the model.

What Nobody Told You

Nobody told you the real definition of an asset

In this book, an asset is one thing: something that earns without your hours. That single test disqualifies most of what the world sells you as assets. The car is a costume. The watch is a costume. The wardrobe, the trim on the truck, the points on the card, costumes.

Even your primary home is mostly a liability wearing an asset costume: it takes money every month and pays you in shelter and appreciation you cannot eat. This is not an argument against owning a home. It is an argument against counting it as your wealth engine and calling yourself an investor because you sleep inside your net worth.

Nobody told you what the real menu looks like

There are only a few true asset families, and none of them require a trust fund to enter. A business with systems, one that can produce value for a customer without you personally in the room, is the highest-leverage family and the hardest. Equity, ownership slices of businesses, whether index funds bought boringly every month or shares in something you helped build, is the most accessible family. Real estate that cash flows, bought on math instead of emotion, is the family with the most tax advantages attached, and Chapter 14 goes deep. And intellectual property, a book, a course, a product, software, something built once that sells while you sleep, is the family with the lowest entry cost and the highest tolerance for starting small. You do not need all four. You need one, started, this year.

Nobody told you that boring is a feature

The asset that changes your life at 45 looks embarrassingly small at 32. The first index fund contribution is a rounding error. The first rental cash flows a few hundred dollars. The first product makes coffee money. Every real portfolio I have ever admired started as something the owner would have been mildly embarrassed to show off, and that is precisely why most people never start: they are shopping for an impressive asset when they should be planting a boring one. The Flexer from Chapter 20 cannot do this chapter. Boring compounds. Impressive depreciates.

Nobody told you the ownership math on time

Run one honest calculation. Take your age, assume you work to 65, and count your remaining earning hours: roughly 2,000 a year times the years left. That is your entire inventory. Every hour sold is gone. Now notice what an asset does: it adds hours you do not have to live. A rental property works 24 hours a day. An index fund compounds on Sundays. A book sells while you are at your kid's game.

Assets are how a human being gets more than 24 hours in a day, and they are the only way. You cannot out-hustle this math. You can only out-own it.

And nobody told you that your first asset changes you before it changes your balance sheet

The dollar amounts start small, but the identity shift is immediate and enormous. The first time money arrives that you did not trade an hour for, something in your Q1 programming breaks, permanently, in the best way. Ownership stops being something other people do. You stop reading about the game and you are in it. The gap between zero assets and one small asset is a different life. The gap between one and five is just math.

One modern addendum, because someone in your group chat will raise it: speculative assets, crypto included, are not banned from the club, they are simply sized by the same two filters as everything else. If it fails the earning test, it earns nothing while you hold it, then it is a speculation, not an asset, and speculations get position sizes your survivability can shrug off at zero. Own it if you choose, sized so that being wrong is a story and not a setback, and never confuse it with the A that this chapter is building.

The C.A.T. Breakdown

C: Assets are bought with the gap, which is why Chapter 4 came first. No gap, no acquisitions, and the answer to no gap is both ends: control the out, and MMM the in. But there is a C-discipline inside A too: every asset has its own cash flow truth. A rental has a real monthly number after vacancy, maintenance, and reserves, not the fantasy number from the listing. A business has a real owner's take after the business's own reserves. People lose assets they were smart enough to buy because they ran them on fantasy cash flow. Run the truth layer on everything you own, not just on yourself.

A: Pick your first family deliberately, using two filters. Filter one: proximity. The best first asset sits near something you already know, your industry, your skill, your unfair advantage, because knowledge you already own lowers the tuition. Filter two: survivability. Your first asset must be sized so that its complete failure does not end you. First assets are partly education, and education you cannot survive is not education, it is a Goofball chapter story. Small, near, and real beats big, far, and impressive every single time.

T: Here is where the letters lock together, because the tax code is not neutral about this chapter. The code is written by and for owners, and it says so on every page. Hour-renters get a W-2 and a handful of deductions. Owners get depreciation, expense deductions, retirement plans with much higher ceilings, capital gains rates instead of ordinary rates, 1031 exchanges, QSBS, step-up in basis, the ability to pay their kids legally. I am not editorializing about whether that is fair. I am telling you the rules of the game you are already standing in. Every asset family comes with its own tax playbook, and choosing assets without knowing the playbook is leaving money on every table you sit at. The code rewards owners. Become one and collect.

The Quarter Lens

Q1: A child who watches a parent own something, even something tiny, gets a template installed that no course can replicate later. If you are a parent, your side asset is a curriculum.

Q2: The planting quarter, and the math is not emotional, it is brutal. Assets bought in Q2 get twenty to forty years of compounding. The same dollars deployed in Q3 get half the runway, and no future income buys the years back. Q2 is also when the Flexer competes hardest for the gap, which is why so many people arrive at 40 with a great story and no Schedule E. If you are in Q2: plant now, plant boring, plant near.

Q3: The stacking quarter. Peak income plus existing assets equals acceleration, and Q3 owners get to make offense decisions: scale the business, add doors, concentrate or diversify. Q3 non-owners face the honest conversation this book exists to prevent, and the answer even then is the same, start now, smaller runway beats no runway.

Q4: Assets convert from growth engines to income and protection. The questions become sequence, risk, and structure, all of them easier for people who spent decades as owners and know how their machines behave.

Overtime: Assets are what transfer. Hours die with the worker. This is the bluntest sentence in the book and I am leaving it in.

The Move to Make Now

Three moves, thirty days.

One: take inventory. List everything you own that passes the test, earns without your hours. Short honest list beats long flattering one. Zero is a fine starting score; it is only a bad ending score.

Two: choose your first family, on paper, using the two filters: nearest to what you know, survivable if it fails. Write one paragraph: my first or next asset is X, it costs roughly Y to start, and its job is Z dollars a month by this date. Vague intentions buy nothing.

Three: automate the most accessible family regardless of what you chose. A monthly automatic investment into a boring, diversified fund, sized to your gap, starting this week. This is not the whole strategy. It is the floor, the thing that guarantees that whatever else happens, you exit every year owning more than you entered it.

And one subtraction: identify the largest monthly payment currently building someone else's asset, and shrink or kill it. Fund the plant with the pruning.

The Warning

Two frauds will visit you the moment you decide to become an owner, and I need you ready for both.

The first fraud is external: the opportunity seller. The moment you have a gap and intention, the pitches find you, the deal from the guy at the gym, the can't-miss thing your cousin is raising for, the course selling passive income in 90 days. Run every pitch through the letters and through Chapter 20. Real assets survive boring questions: show me the actual cash flow, the actual tax treatment, the actual downside. Fake assets need urgency, and urgency is the tell. Your friends do not need access to your money to cost you money, and neither do strangers with a deck.

The second fraud is internal: the researcher. He reads about assets for years. He compares platforms, watches videos, optimizes a plan for money he has not deployed. Research is the Office Rat version of ownership, all the feeling of progress, none of the equity. At some point, and the point is this month, you buy the boring thing and become an owner of record. Nobody cares more than you will, and nobody can plant it for you.

The Checklist

☐ Complete the asset inventory using the one test: earns without my hours

☐ Choose your first asset family using the proximity and survivability filters

☐ Write the one-paragraph asset thesis: what, cost to start, job, date

☐ Automate a monthly investment into a diversified fund, starting this week

☐ Kill or shrink the largest payment building someone else's asset

The Before 40 Club Rule

Hours die with the worker. Own something that works when you do not, and start while it is still embarrassing.

One question before you go. What do I own that earns when I am not in the room?

Put this chapter to work in the companion Before 40 Club Workbook at before4oclub.com.

CHAPTER 6:

TAX PLANNING: APRIL IS TOO LATE

"A tax refund is an interest-free loan you gave the government."

The Expensive Lesson

There are two kinds of people in my office every spring, and they are separated by one word.

The first kind arrives in April with a shoebox, literal or digital, and a question: what do I owe? For this person, everything is already decided. The income landed how it landed. The entity is whatever it is. The accounts got funded or did not. The records exist or do not. My job with this person is archaeology: dig up the year, report it accurately, and deliver a verdict. They call this doing their taxes, and every option that could have changed the number died on December 31 while they were at a party.

The second kind of person talked to me in June. And September. And November. For this person, the year was still alive: income could be timed, the election could be made, the accounts could be funded, the purchase could land on the right side of the calendar, the records were built as the year happened. Same tax code, same government, same deadlines. Completely different bills, year after year, compounding.

The first person files. The second person plans. Filing is recording history. Planning is writing it. And the expensive lesson of this chapter is that the difference between those two people is not income, sophistication, or connections. It is a calendar. April is too late, and it has always been too late, and the entire tax preparation industry is built around servicing people who show up after the game ends and asking them if they want to do anything differently, next year, which they say yes to, and then do not.

You are done being the first person. This chapter is the conversion.

The Story

Here is the tale of two clients, and the only variable between them is a calendar. The first kind arrives on April first: hey Busayo, I need help filing. At that point there are exactly three moves left on the board: file the return, file an extension, and adjust the W-4 going forward. That is it. Every real option died on December thirty-first while we were not talking.

The second kind calls in May, June, July, August: Busayo, I am expecting a windfall. I am exiting this position. I am selling my company. How do we model this distribution? Same caliber of person, sometimes the same income level, completely different outcome, because now the whole board is live. On one side of my ledger sits a client I saved close to one hundred fifty thousand dollars, and the honest truth is that nothing exotic happened, we simply did the planning while the year was still alive. On the other side sits a client who owed the IRS a painful number for one reason: we did not speak all year. Purely the calendar. That is the whole chapter in two phone calls.

The reason that story matters is that nothing in it required aggression. No gray areas, no schemes, no loopholes from the internet. Just the same rulebook, read before the game instead of after. That is the whole discipline, and it is available to anyone willing to move one conversation from April to June.

What Nobody Told You

Nobody told you the code is instructions, not a verdict

The tax code is enormous because it is full of if-then statements written directly to you. If you save for retirement in this account, then this money is not taxed now. If you own a business and keep these records, then these costs reduce your income. If you hold this asset this long, then this cheaper rate applies. If you structure this entity this way from day one, then this exit gets this treatment. Every one of those sentences is the government telling you, in writing, how to pay less, legally, on purpose. The people you resent for paying less tax are, overwhelmingly, just people who read their mail. Take the rewards that are printed in the rules. Leave the fantasies.

Nobody told you the difference between a preparer and a planner

A preparer is a historian: accurate, necessary, and structurally incapable of saving you money on a year that is already over. A planner is a strategist who works mid-year, when the moves are alive. Most people have a preparer and believe they have a planner, and the belief costs them every single year. Here is the test: if your tax professional has never contacted you between May and December with a move to make, you have a historian. Historians are fine. Just stop expecting history to change.

Nobody told you that the entity myth eats a generation of business owners

Say it with me, because it is the flag of this book: your LLC did not save you taxes. Your structure might. A basic LLC is taxed exactly like you with no LLC. It is a legal container, and containers do not create savings. What moves the number is what runs inside the container: the S election made at the right income level, not before, because below that level the payroll cost eats the savings. The reasonable salary, set defensibly, not at the internet's favorite fantasy number. Clean books, a payment rhythm, records that survive questions. The container is the beginning of the sentence. Most people stop there and frame the certificate.

Nobody told you that timing is a strategy all by itself

The same dollar, moved across a calendar line, changes its tax life. Income accelerated into a low year or deferred out of a high one. The equipment purchase landing in the year that needs the deduction. The account funded before its deadline instead of after. The asset held past the line where the cheaper rate begins. The election filed inside its 30-day window instead of discovered in year three, which is a one-page form that has decided seven-figure outcomes. None of this is exotic. All of it dies in April. Timing is the cheapest tax strategy in existence, and its only price is paying attention while the year is alive.

Nobody told you that records are money

Not for the audit fantasy people fear, but for the daily reality: a deduction you cannot support is a deduction you either do not take, losing real money, or take nervously, buying real risk. Clean books beat clever deductions, every year, forever. The business owner with boring, current, accurate records takes everything the rules allow, calmly, and sleeps. The one with a shoebox takes a guess. Recordkeeping is not administration. It is the licensing requirement for every strategy in this chapter.

And nobody told you where the line is

So let me draw it, because the internet keeps smudging it. Avoidance is legal: using the written rules to pay the minimum the law requires. That is not cheating; that is literacy, and judges have said so for a century. Evasion is illegal: hiding income, faking deductions, lying on the form. And in between lives the gray-area pitch, the scheme that arrives with a wink, sold by someone who will not be sitting next to you when the letter comes. The rule of this book: if a strategy only works when nobody looks at it closely, it is not a strategy, it is a countdown. There is more than enough money in the boring, written, black-letter moves. I have built a career proving it.

The C.A.T. Breakdown

C: Tax planning starts as a cash flow discipline, and Chapter 4 already installed the plumbing: the reserve percentage on every untaxed dollar, estimated payments on a quarterly rhythm instead of an annual heart attack, and the W-4 tuned so April is a shrug. Add one number to your dashboard: your effective rate, total tax divided by total income, known by heart. It is the price you pay to play, and people who know their price start finding it negotiable.

A: Every asset family from Chapter 5 ships with its own tax playbook, and buying the asset without the playbook wastes half the point. Real estate ships with depreciation, the paper loss that shelters real cash flow, and the 1031, and eventually the step-up. Equity ships with capital gains rates, loss harvesting, and, for founders and early employees, QSBS, the provision that can make millions of exit gain federally tax-free if, and only if, the structure was right years before the exit. Businesses ship with the richest playbook of all: deductions, retirement plans with owner-sized ceilings, the ability to employ your kids legally, and entity elections. Owners get the good pages of the rulebook. This is the T reason the A chapter exists.

T: The discipline itself is a calendar, not an event. A real tax year has a rhythm: a mid-year review while everything is still movable, a fall check as the picture firms up, a December session for the last live decisions, and then filing season as a formality, because the return was decided months earlier. Put the rhythm on your actual calendar this week. Planning that lives in intentions attends the funeral in April with everyone else.

The Quarter Lens

Q1: Nobody teaches children taxes, which is why every quarter after Q1 experiences them as ambush. A teenager with a working papers job and a custodial Roth is receiving a better tax education than most adults ever get.

Q2: The structure quarter. Entity chosen right, elections filed on time, retirement accounts opened and automated, the planner relationship established while the numbers are small and mistakes are cheap. Q2 tax planning looks unimpressive and is worth the most, because structure decisions made here, especially for anyone building a business or holding equity, echo for decades. The exit you might have at 45 is being taxed right now, at 31, by paperwork you have not thought about.

Q3: The ammunition quarter. Peak income makes every planning move worth more, and the sophisticated plays, defined benefit plans, timing strategies, asset location, real estate stacking, earn their keep. Q3 with a planner is harvest. Q3 with a historian is the most expensive decade of a person's life, invisibly.

Q4: The order-of-operations quarter. Which account gets drawn first, when benefits start, how the brackets get managed in the gap years: drawdown sequencing is a tax discipline that routinely swings six figures over a retirement, and it is decided well by people who arrive with structure.

Overtime: The transfer quarter, where basis step-up, beneficiary designations, and titling decide whether what you built moves intact or gets carved. Chapter 13 and the Overtime close carry it. One sentence here: the largest tax mistakes in death are made by the living, earlier, through silence.

The Move to Make Now

Four moves, this month.

One: read your own scoreboard. Last year's full return, thirty minutes, and compute your effective rate. Write it down. That number is your baseline, and this chapter's job in your life is to bend it.

Two: classify your professional. Historian or strategist, using the test above. If historian, your assignment is one conversation: ask directly, do you do mid-year planning, and what would that look like for me? The answer sorts everything.

Three: put the rhythm on the calendar. A June planning session, a September check, a December decision meeting. Recurring, named, real.

Four: if you own a business or any income arrives untaxed, verify the foundation in writing: reserve account funded by automatic percentage, estimated payment dates on the calendar, books current within 30 days, entity and any elections reviewed against your actual income level, by a professional, dated this year. If you hold or expect equity in anything, add one line: ask specifically about the exit provisions, because those clocks start at formation, not at sale.

The Warning

Two failure modes, opposite directions, same cost.

The first is the one this whole chapter fights: passivity. Deciding this is all above you, handing the shoebox over every April, and paying the ignorance tax annually, forever. It compounds exactly like an asset, against you.

The second is overcorrection: becoming the Genius from Chapter 20. He discovers tax strategy at 2am, and within a month he is quoting provisions at parties, structuring things he does not understand, and buying vehicles for deductions on businesses with no profit. Do not buy the truck for the write-off. A deduction is a discount on something you spend; it is never a reason to spend. The Genius turns a keeping-more discipline into a spending-more hobby and calls it strategy. The boring middle, written rules, real planner, live calendar, clean records, is where all the money actually is. No one is bigger than the program, especially the recently enlightened.

The Checklist

☐ Compute and write down last year's effective tax rate

☐ Classify your tax professional: historian or strategist, using the mid-year contact test

☐ Schedule the rhythm: June, September, and December sessions, recurring

☐ Verify the foundation: reserve automated, estimated dates calendared, books current

☐ Confirm your entity and elections match your actual income level, reviewed this year

The Before 40 Club Rule

Filing records history. Planning writes it. Be the person whose April is a formality.

One question before you go. Is my tax professional a historian or a strategist, and how do I know?

Put this chapter to work in the companion Before 40 Club Workbook at before40club.com.

PART II:
THE EXAMS

Nine chapters, nine scheduled exams: marriage, the house, the kids, the business, the IRS letter, the trap, the family, the rental, the equity. Each one is a life moment that is secretly a money exam, graded on preparation done months or years earlier. You do not have to read these in order. Read the one arriving next in your life first.

CHAPTER 7:

BEFORE YOU GET MARRIED

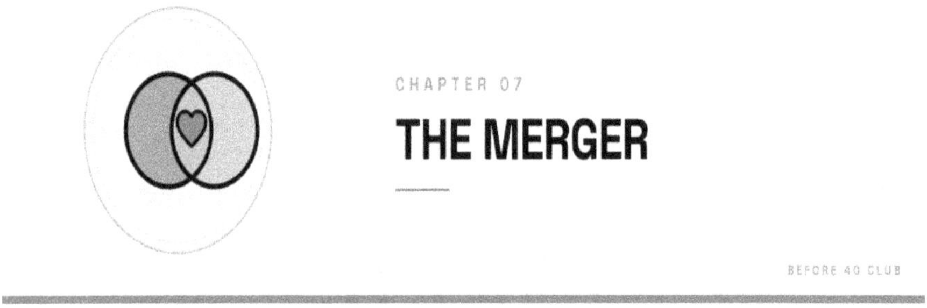

The Expensive Lesson

You are planning a wedding. The IRS is processing a merger.

Both events happen on the same day, and only one of them gets any planning. Couples will spend fourteen months and a small fortune choosing flowers, venues, and a playlist, and zero structured hours on the fact that they are about to combine two credit histories, two debt loads, two tax lives, two sets of Q1 programming, and two definitions of the word normal into a single financial entity, with the state as a witness and the tax code as the operating agreement they never read.

Here is the number nobody puts on the invitation: money is one of the most reliable sources of conflict in a marriage, and in nearly every money fight I have ever heard described across a desk, the fight was installed before the wedding, in the conversations that never happened. Not caused by the marriage. Imported into it, with the tags still on.

The expensive lesson: marriage is love, and it is also a financial merger, and mergers that skip due diligence do not skip the consequences, they just discover them later, with interest, in front of a mediator. Every business merger on earth begins with disclosure: here is what I own, here is what I owe, here is how I operate, here is what I am afraid of. Two people who claim to love each other deserve at least the diligence two companies that do not love each other would perform. This chapter is that diligence, in plain English, and it is the cheapest chapter in the book, because everything in it is free and everything it prevents is not.

The Story

A couple came to me after the wedding, and the surprise was already joint property. One spouse carried old tax debt and credit card debt, money owed to the IRS from a life the other spouse had never audited, and now they were married filing jointly, which meant the balance sheet had merged even though the conversation never had. I have seen the business version too: a return both spouses signed, where one partner's massive tax bill became a household problem the other partner learned about from me.

So I now run the meeting this chapter is built on, and I will be honest, it is an awkward ninety minutes. Old debts, alimony and child support realities, the 529 questions, the filing status math, what I call pre-marriage tax planning, which is not marriage counseling, it is cheaper and it prevents some of the need for it. Understand what you are actually doing at the altar: you are merging the house, the retirement accounts, the business interests, the equity, every financial investment either of you holds. And if the merger ever unwinds, it does not unwind by walking away. It unwinds through equalization payments and divorce attorneys. Have the awkward ninety minutes with your CPA before the wedding, not your financial advisor after it. The couple who did it with me bought themselves years of never being surprised.

What stays with me from every version of that story is the same detail: the information was always available before the wedding. Nothing was hidden, exactly. It was just never asked, because asking felt unromantic. Let me reframe that word permanently. There is nothing romantic about a garnished refund. Diligence is not distrust. Diligence is what you do when you intend for something to last.

What Nobody Told You

Nobody told you that your filing status is a decision, not a default

Married filing jointly is not automatic and not always right. Jointly usually wins on pure rate math and unlocks credits that separately forfeits. But jointly also means joint and several liability: both names on the return means both people own the whole return, its accuracy, its balance, its problems, regardless of whose income created them. Separately costs money in most years but builds a wall, and there are real situations where the wall is worth the toll: a spouse with income-driven student loan payments calculated off joint income, a spouse with tax trouble in motion, a business with question marks. The point is not which one. The point is that it is a real decision with real numbers, run both ways, every year, on purpose.

Nobody told you that you can marry a tax debt

If your future spouse owes the IRS from before the wedding, that debt does not become legally yours, but its consequences move in with you. File jointly and the refund you were both counting on can be applied to their old balance while you watch. There is a form for the injured spouse in exactly this situation, and there is relief for spouses genuinely deceived on a joint return, but every one of those remedies is cleanup. The prevention costs one sentence, asked before the wedding: is there anything unfiled, unpaid, or unresolved with the IRS or the state? Ask it with love. Ask it anyway. The answer changes nothing about the wedding and everything about the plan.

Nobody told you that marriage changes your paycheck immediately

The W-4 conversation from Chapter 4 arrives here with a ring on. Two incomes, newly married, both withholding as if the other does not exist, is the single most common surprise tax bill among newlyweds: two salaries stack into higher brackets while two paychecks withhold like singles. The fix is ten minutes and a worksheet in the first month of marriage. Almost nobody does it, and the first joint April becomes the first joint fight, over a bill that was never necessary.

Nobody told you what to do when one of you owns a business

A business-owning spouse changes the entire merger. Their income is lumpy, their taxes are estimated, their return is complicated, and if you file jointly, you are signing it. The non-owner spouse needs literacy, not control: what the entity is, roughly what it makes, whether the reserve from Chapter 4 exists, whether the estimated payments are actually happening, and who the professional is. You do not need to run the business. You need to never be surprised by it. Surprised is the thing joint filers do not get to be, legally.

Nobody told you that a prenup is financial architecture, not a bet against the marriage

Strip the movie drama off it. A prenup is two adults deciding, while they like each other, what belongs to whom, what stays separate, what becomes joint, and how a worst case would be handled, instead of delegating those decisions to state default rules and future lawyers billing hourly during the worst year of their lives. It matters most when someone brings a business, expects an inheritance, carries significant assets or debts, or has children from before. And even where no document gets signed, the conversation underneath it, what is mine, what is yours, what is ours, is mandatory. Couples who cannot have that conversation are not protecting the romance. They are postponing the invoice.

Nobody told you what the unwind actually costs, so let me, gently

I hope you never need this section, and I refuse to publish a merger chapter without it, because I have watched the unwind from across the desk and it is the most expensive financial event most people ever experience. When a marriage ends, the finances do not end with a conversation. They end in family court, and family court is a financial authority with power most people never imagined: it divides the assets, it can order the sale of the prized possessions, it splits retirement accounts through specialized orders, and it attaches obligations to your future income, child support and spousal support, that function exactly like the liens Chapter 21 will warn you about, court-ordered cash flow commitments that do not care what your retirement date was, arriving monthly for years or decades.

The tax mechanics of the unwind get decided at signature time, when almost nobody is thinking about taxes: the filing status change, who claims head of household, who claims the children and in which years, how the retirement split is papered so it does not trigger a tax bill, and how support payments are treated under current law, which changed for newer agreements and is precisely the kind of detail that belongs in front of a CPA before anything is signed. And the money above all of it: two households now run on income that was sized for one, plus the professional fees, and every dollar of that math is easier when the merger documents from this chapter, the disclosure, the architecture, the prenup as operating agreement, were done with love years earlier. Plan the merger like it will last forever, and paper it like adults who know that some mergers do not.

And nobody told you to run the operating system merge

Chapter 2 gave each of you a money autobiography, and marriage is where two autobiographies try to share one checking account. One of you was installed with money is survived, the other with money is enjoyed, and neither of you is wrong, you are programmed, and unexamined programming does not compromise, it collides. There are three workable account architectures, yours-mine-ours with agreed contributions, fully joint with agreed autonomy thresholds, and fully separate with a shared bills engine, and successful marriages run all three. What the failed ones share is not the architecture. It is that the architecture was never chosen, just defaulted into, and defaults, as always, are the most expensive setting.

The C.A.T. Breakdown

C: The merged truth layer. Before the wedding, or this month if the wedding already happened, build the joint version of Chapter 4: both real take-homes, both real spend patterns from actual statements, the combined gap, and the chosen account architecture with every recurring bill assigned an owner. Then set the two numbers that prevent ninety percent of money fights: the autonomy threshold, the amount either of you can spend without a conversation, and the conversation threshold, the amount that requires one. Couples do not fight about money. They fight about surprises.

A: The merged asset map and the merged liability map, on one page: what each of you owns, owes, and is building, with beneficiaries reviewed, because the person named on your retirement account from a job in 2016 is who gets it, regardless of your vows. Then the offense question, because marriage is not just risk management: two gaps pointed at the same asset thesis build roughly twice as fast, and a couple that plants a first asset together in year one installs a partnership default that compounds for decades. The merger is supposed to be an upgrade. Aim it like one.

T: The four filings of year one. First, the filing status analysis, run both ways, with the loan-payment and liability angles on the table, not just the rate math. Second, both W-4s, adjusted in month one. Third, the disclosure conversation: anything unfiled, unpaid, or in motion, surfaced before it becomes jointly discovered. Fourth, if a business is anywhere in the merger, the estimated-payment rhythm verified and the reserve confirmed. None of this is exotic. All of it is skipped, annually, by millions of otherwise intelligent people in love.

The Quarter Lens

Q2: Most mergers happen here, which is exactly why this is a Before 40 chapter. A Q2 marriage with the diligence done becomes a two-engine build for the exact decades when compounding pays most. A Q2 marriage without it spends those same decades discovering each other's balance sheets by ambush.

Q3: Second marriages and later marriages live here, and they merge more: real assets, real businesses, kids from before, sometimes real debts. Everything in this chapter applies with the volume turned up, and the prenup conversation moves from advisable to nearly mandatory, because the default state rules were not written for your actual family.

Q4 and Overtime: The merger's final exam is titling, beneficiaries, and survivorship, whether the structure you built transfers to the person you built it with, cleanly, or hands them a probate project in their worst year. Deciding it now is a love language. Chapter 13 continues this.

The Move to Make Now

One meeting. Ninety minutes. Calendar it within two weeks, whether the wedding is ahead of you or behind you.

The agenda, in order: full disclosure, every account, every debt, every obligation, anything unfiled or unresolved, no reactions allowed during the read, questions after. Then the architecture decision: yours-mine-ours, joint, or separate-with-engine, chosen out loud. Then the two thresholds, autonomy and conversation, with numbers attached. Then the four filings: status analysis scheduled, W-4s adjusted, beneficiaries reviewed, business rhythm verified if one exists. Close with each of you naming your money default from Chapter 2 and the one behavior the other person should expect under stress.

Ninety minutes. It will be awkward for about eleven of them. It is the highest-yield meeting in this entire book.

The Warning

The failure mode of this chapter is not disagreement. Couples survive disagreement. The failure mode is the performance of agreement: nodding through the meeting, keeping the real account private, softening the debt number, we will figure it out as a plan. Hear this in the plainest voice I have: in a joint filing, in a shared household, in a merged life, a financial secret is not privacy, it is a liability accruing in your partner's name without their signature. And a misaligned person is an expensive liability, but a misinformed partner is one you created.

And the second warning, for the diligent one in the couple, because there is always a diligent one: this chapter is not a weapon. It is not for auditing your partner into compliance or scoring their Q1 programming against yours. Purpose comes first, and the purpose of the merger is the life, not the spreadsheet. Run the diligence like a partner, not a regulator. The goal is two people who are never surprised, not one person who is always right.

The Checklist

☐ Schedule the 90-minute merger meeting within two weeks

☐ Complete mutual full disclosure: accounts, debts, obligations, anything unfiled or unresolved

☐ Choose the account architecture out loud: yours-mine-ours, joint, or separate-with-engine

☐ Set the autonomy threshold and the conversation threshold, with numbers

☐ Adjust both W-4s in month one of marriage

The Before 40 Club Rule

The wedding is one day. The merger is the rest of your life. Plan them in that proportion.

One question before you go. What money conversation are we still avoiding, and what is the avoidance costing?

Put this chapter to work in the companion Before 40 Club Workbook at before40club.com.

CHAPTER 8:

BEFORE YOU BUY THE HOUSE

The Expensive Lesson

The bank told you what you can borrow. Nobody told you what you can afford. Those are two different numbers, and the gap between them is where house-poor lives.

Here is how the trap is built, step by step, and notice that no one in the sequence is your enemy. The lender approves you for the maximum the formulas allow, because lending is their product. The agent shows you homes at the top of that approval, because commission follows price. The listing gets staged to sell a feeling, because feelings sign contracts. And then you, armed with a pre-approval letter and a Saturday afternoon, fall in love with a monthly payment that was calculated by people who will never pay it.

The approval number answers one question: what is the most this person can carry before the math legally breaks. That is not a recommendation. That is a ceiling, and nobody furnishes their life against the ceiling on purpose. Yet that is exactly what most first-time buyers do, and then they spend the next decade discovering that the mortgage was never the cost. The mortgage was the entry fee.

The expensive lesson of this chapter, the line I want playing in your head at every open house: the house is not the flex. Keeping the house, comfortably, while still building assets and still sleeping at night, is the flex. The bank tells you the max. C.A.T. tells you the right number. This chapter is how you find it before you sign anything.

The Story

I have watched both versions of this exam. The house-poor version: the client eyeing the one and a half million dollar home, fully approved, taking the approval as permission, and then meeting the second-year reassessment and everything else the true monthly cost had been hiding. Qualifying was never the question. The question was whether the cash flow could carry it and stay calm, and nobody at the closing table gets paid to ask that one.

The self-employed version is the quieter heartbreak. Clients denied mortgages because years of aggressive write-offs, often inherited from a previous preparer, had shrunk their paper income, and paper income is the only income a lender can see. The rebuild takes two clean, complete, accurate years of returns, plus the CPA letter, and there is no shortcut through it, which is why the self-employed sit this exam two years before the open house. And my own honest position, since this book promised you honesty: I am personally not big on buying a primary residence, because I think in cash flow, and I price the maintenance, the taxes, and the carrying costs the way this chapter taught you to. That is not a rule for you. It is proof that I run my own numbers through the same machine I am handing you, and that the right answer is the one the true monthly cost approves, not the one the approval letter does.

Every version of that story shares one root: the decision was made on the listing price and the mortgage payment, two numbers that together describe maybe two-thirds of the real cost. The last third arrives after closing, monthly, forever, and it arrives whether you planned for it or not. Planning for it is the whole chapter.

What Nobody Told You

Nobody told you the true monthly cost

The mortgage payment is the headline. The truth is the mortgage plus property taxes, which reassess and rise and in some counties rival the mortgage itself, plus insurance, which has been repricing upward almost everywhere, plus maintenance, which runs one to two percent of the home's value every year whether you see it or not, because the roof is aging in silence, plus utilities scaled to the bigger space, plus the reserves a homeowner must carry that a renter never thinks about. Add those lines before you shop, not after you close. A house you can afford is one whose true monthly cost fits inside your real take-home with the gap still alive. If the gap dies to buy the house, you did not buy an asset. You bought a beautiful cage.

Nobody told you not to drain every dollar at closing

The down payment conversation swallows people whole. They scrape every account to hit a number, and they arrive at closing technically homeowners and functionally broke. Closing is not the finish line. It is the starting line, and the first year of ownership is the most expensive year: the moving costs, the furniture the old place never needed, the repairs the inspection called minor, the surprise the inspection missed entirely. The rule: you do not buy the house unless, the day after closing, you still hold reserves covering months of the true monthly cost. If hitting the down payment kills the reserve, the answer is not a smaller reserve. It is a smaller house or a later date. The market will still be there. Your liquidity might not.

Nobody told you how to build the first down payment, or how big it actually has to be

Twenty percent is a tradition, not a law, and treating it as a law keeps people renting for a decade past necessary. Here is the real math. Conventional loans commonly close with far less down, and first-time buyer programs, FHA loans, and state assistance programs exist specifically for this moment. Below twenty percent you will usually carry PMI, private mortgage insurance, a monthly fee for the lender's risk, and PMI is not a moral failure. It is a line item. Price it. In many markets, a smaller down payment plus PMI plus five extra years of ownership and appreciation beats five more years of saving toward a tradition. Run both versions on paper and let the numbers pick. Now the sourcing rules, because where the down payment comes from matters as much as its size. It comes from the gap, accumulated on purpose in its own named account, fed automatically every month the moment the house becomes a real goal. It can come from documented gifts, which lenders allow with a paper trail. It does not come from the emergency reserve, because closing on a house while deleting your safety net is how homeowners become sellers. It does not come from raiding retirement accounts, because a dollar pulled from compounding in Q2 costs your Q4 several dollars, plus possible taxes and penalties for the privilege. And it does not come from new debt, because lenders will find it and price you for it. Two years out, open the account and name it. Eighteen months out, automate the number. Twelve months out, get the credit file clean and stop opening anything. That is the whole program: boring, dated, and automatic, like everything else in this book that works.

Nobody told the self-employed that their tax strategy fights their mortgage

This is the collision nobody warns business owners about, and it lands in my office every spring. All year, Chapter 6 has you legally maximizing deductions to lower taxable income. Then you apply for a mortgage, and the lender underwrites you on that same taxable income, the small number you worked so hard to create. The write-offs that saved you tax just shrank you on paper, and the denial letter does not explain the irony. The fix is not fake income and it is not abandoning planning. The fix is a calendar: if a purchase is twelve to twenty-four months out, you and your tax professional plan the returns with the mortgage in mind, two clean, coherent years that tell a lender the true story. Approval is a document exam, and the self-employed sit it two years early or repeat it.

Nobody told you to decide the structure before the offer

Personal name or entity is a before question, not an after question. For the home you will live in, personal ownership wins almost every time: the financing is better, the tax treatment of a primary residence is a genuine gift, including the exclusion of a large slice of gain when you sell a home you have lived in long enough, and an LLC around your own residence usually adds cost and complexity while subtracting benefits. For an investment property, the calculus changes completely, and Chapter 14 owns that ground. The point here is sequencing: the title question, the how-we-hold-this-as-a-couple question, and the what-does-this-do-to-our-April question all get answered before you are emotionally committed to a kitchen.

Nobody told you how the house changes your tax return

The first April after buying is a small education. The property taxes and mortgage interest may or may not actually change your bill, depending on whether they lift you past the standard deduction, and plenty of buyers who were promised huge tax benefits by someone at a barbecue discover the standard deduction was already doing the work. Escrow will move, taxes will reassess, and if you married the house and a marriage in the same year, the W-4 from Chapter 7 needs its second visit. None of this is bad news. All of it is news, and news is better received in June than discovered in April.

And nobody told you to stress-test the purchase

One question, asked while you still have the pen and not the keys: if our income dropped for three months, do we keep this house without panic? Job loss, a slow quarter in the business, a medical stretch, a leave. If the honest answer is no, the true cost is too high, whatever the approval letter says. You are not buying for the best-case year. You are buying for the median year and surviving the worst one. The stress test is free. Skipping it is not.

The C.A.T. Breakdown

C: The house is the largest recurring line your cash flow will ever carry, so it gets sized by the truth layer, not the approval letter. Compute the true monthly cost, subtract it from your real take-home, and look at what remains: if the gap from Chapter 4 does not survive the purchase, the purchase fails C, full stop, regardless of how it photographs. And build the homeowner reserve as its own assignment: a dedicated account, fed monthly, sized to the one-to-two-percent maintenance reality, so the water heater is an errand instead of an emergency.

A: Your primary home is shelter first and an asset costume second, and buying it with asset language is how people overpay. It does not cash flow. It consumes. Its appreciation is real but locked, and you live inside it, which makes it the one asset you can never sell without disrupting your whole life. The A discipline here is a single guardrail: the house must not eat the asset budget. If the true monthly cost consumes the entire gap, you have traded twenty years of Chapter 5 for granite countertops, and no one who has done that recommends it by year ten. Buy the house that leaves the factory running.

T: Run the tax picture before the offer: what the interest and property taxes actually do against your standard deduction, what the escrowed taxes look like after reassessment rather than at the seller's old rate, what the primary residence exclusion means for your long game, and, for the self-employed, whether the last two returns tell a story a lender will fund. And keep the closing documents forever, because the basis you establish today, plus every improvement receipt you keep along the way, is the number that protects you at the sale decades from now. Recordkeeping on a house is a savings account with a very long maturity.

The Quarter Lens

Q2: The first-house quarter, and the pressure quarter. Everyone around you is buying, the feed is full of keys and doormats, and waiting feels like losing. Hear the reframe: in Q2, buying right beats buying now. A Q2 house bought at the right number accelerates everything, forced savings, stability, a base to build from. A Q2 house bought at the ceiling delays every other chapter in this book by a decade. The market rewards patience unevenly, but your balance sheet rewards it every time.

Q3: The upgrade quarter, and the trap has better lighting. Peak income arrives and whispers that you have earned the bigger house, and maybe you have, but run the same stress test at the new scale, because a Q3 income locked into a maximum house becomes a cage exactly when career risk peaks. Q3 is also when the house-rich, cash-poor pattern hardens: enormous equity, thin liquidity, and options shrinking. Equity you cannot access without moving is comfort, not strategy.

Q4: The house becomes a question again: keep, downsize, or convert. The primary residence exclusion, the step-up rules, and the property taxes on a fixed income all move to the front. Q4 handles this well when Q2 and Q3 kept records and kept liquidity.

Overtime: The house is often the largest asset in the estate and the easiest one to fumble in transfer. Titling and basis, decided now, spare your family the version of this chapter with lawyers in it.

The Move to Make Now

If a purchase is anywhere on your horizon, run the pre-flight this month, in this order.

One: build the true monthly cost on the actual houses you are browsing, all six lines, mortgage, taxes at reassessed rates, insurance quoted for real, maintenance percentage, utilities, reserve contribution. Two: set your number, the true monthly cost your real take-home carries with the gap intact, and write it down before you attend a single showing, because the number you set at a desk survives contact with a staged kitchen and the number you set in the kitchen does not. Three: confirm the day-after-closing reserve, months of true cost, untouched by the down payment. Four: if self-employed, get your last two returns in front of your tax professional with one question: do these approve, and if not, what does the next return need to look like? Five: run the stress test out loud with whoever is signing beside you.

Already own the home? The chapter still pays: rebuild the true monthly cost at today's rates, check the reserve against the one-to-two-percent reality, and start the improvement-receipt file this week if it does not exist.

The Warning

The pressure on this purchase will not come from lenders. It will come from people you love and strangers you follow. The parents asking when. The feed converting a financing decision into a personality trait. The renting-is-throwing-money-away chorus, chanted by people who have never once computed the true monthly cost of their own homes. Renting while your gap builds assets is not throwing money away. It is paying for shelter with one line instead of six while your factory runs. Some years, in some cities, at some prices, the renter with a funded gap is beating the owner with an empty one, and the scoreboard from Chapter 1 will say so even when the feed will not.

And the second warning belongs to the Flexer: the house is the biggest costume in the store. It is the one purchase where ego can borrow thirty years of your future at interest and call it maturity. No one is bigger than the program, and the program says the same thing in every room of every open house: the house is not the flex. Keeping it is.

The Checklist

☐ Open and name the down payment account, automate the monthly feed, and price the smaller-down-plus-PMI version against the twenty percent version on paper

☐ Build the six-line true monthly cost on any house you are considering

☐ Set your number at a desk, in writing, before any showing

☐ Confirm the day-after-closing reserve: months of true cost, separate from the down payment

☐ Self-employed: review the last two returns with your tax professional for approval strength

The Before 40 Club Rule

The bank tells you the max. The truth layer tells you the number. Never confuse the ceiling for the plan.

One question before you go. Does my gap survive the true monthly cost of the home I want?

Put this chapter to work in the companion Before 40 Club Workbook at before40club.com.

CHAPTER 9:

BEFORE YOU HAVE KIDS

The Expensive Lesson

Children are the largest financial decision most people ever make, and the one they make with the least planning. Not the least love. The least planning.

Run the comparison honestly. A house gets an inspection, an appraisal, a lawyer, and thirty pages of disclosures. A car gets a test drive and a payment calculator. A child, the two-decade commitment that reprices your housing, your career flexibility, your insurance, your taxes, your time, and your definition of enough, gets a nursery color scheme and a stroller registry. Nobody runs the numbers, partly because running numbers on a child feels cold, and partly because nobody handed them the numbers to run.

Let me remove the coldness first, because it blocks the whole chapter. Planning for a child financially is not reducing a child to a cost. It is the opposite. It is deciding, in advance, that this person will be raised by parents who are calm about money instead of parents who are cornered by it, in a household where money is a system instead of a recurring emergency. The single greatest financial gift you can give a child is not an account with their name on it. It is a Q1 without money panic in the walls. Chapter 2 taught you that you are still running the atmosphere of your childhood household. This chapter is where you realize you are now the atmosphere.

The expensive lesson: kids do not break budgets. Unplanned kids' expenses break unplanned budgets, on a schedule you could have seen coming, because childhood costs are the most predictable large expenses in existence. Daycare arrives on a known date. School costs arrive annually for years you can count on your fingers. College arrives exactly eighteen years after the birthday. Nothing in this chapter is a surprise. It only behaves like one for families who refuse to look at the calendar.

The Story

I am not a parent yet, and I want you to know that up front, because what follows comes from the desk, not the nursery, and the desk has seen both families this chapter describes. The family who planned before the birth: the accounts opened early, sometimes a 529 seeded by the grandparents, the childcare cost priced before it arrived, the school decision vetted as a real number, the next generation's trust structure already standing. And the family improvising: the daycare bill discovered at full price, the school committed to on emotion, every cost arriving as a surprise that was never actually a surprise.

Here is the phrase I use with clients, and I mean it with all the love in the world: children are lovable liabilities. Most kids are not going to be LeBron James or Henry Kravis. They are going to be wonderful, expensive, and dependent on your planning for a very long time, and pretending otherwise is not optimism, it is a decade of unpriced bills. People love being spontaneous, living la vida loca, and children are precisely the moment that stops being free. You cannot raise children on hope, and you cannot plan for them after they arrive when the whole exam was scheduled nine months in advance. Plan before the birth. That is the entire story.

The gap between those two families was never income. It was lead time. Both had eighteen years of notice. Only one used it, and using it is mostly a matter of doing three or four unglamorous things early, which is the rest of this chapter.

What Nobody Told You

Nobody told you the first-year budget resets everything

Before the child arrives, rebuild the Chapter 4 truth layer as a family of three or four: the childcare line, which in many cities rivals a mortgage, the insurance changes, the gear, the medical costs, and, honestly modeled, the income change if one parent's hours shift. Then resize the emergency reserve to the new monthly reality, because your old reserve was sized for a household that no longer exists. Families do not get wrecked by the baby. They get wrecked by running a new household on an old budget.

Nobody told you the 529 is one of the cleanest tax moves available to a parent

Here is the machine in plain English: you put money in after tax, it grows with no tax on the growth, and when it comes out for qualified education costs, the growth comes out untaxed too. Growth that is never taxed, over eighteen years, is a serious machine, and many states add a deduction or credit on the way in. The mistakes are all timing and titling: waiting, because the whole engine is time, or overfunding so aggressively that the household's own retirement starves, which brings us to the oxygen mask rule below. Start small, start at birth or before, automate it, and let the calendar do the heavy lifting. For families with a windfall or serious income, the code even allows front-loading several years of gifts at once, a move worth a conversation with your professional rather than a guess.

Nobody told you that whose name is on the account changes everything

The instinct is sweet: put money in the kid's name. The consequences are not. A custodial account, the UTMA or UGMA, is an irrevocable gift: at the age your state sets, that money legally belongs to the child, whoever the child turns out to be at twenty-one, and you have no say. Worse for most families, student assets are weighed far more heavily than parent assets in the financial aid formulas, so the loving gift in the kid's name can shrink the aid package it was meant to supplement. A 529 owned by the parent gets gentler aid treatment and keeps the parent in control. The rule of thumb that serves most families: 529 first for education money, custodial accounts only with eyes open, and never park serious money in a child's name for tax cuteness without understanding what you just gave away.

Nobody told you a working teenager can start compounding for retirement

The custodial Roth is the sleeper move of this chapter. A child with real earned income, the summer job, the lifeguarding, the legitimate work in the family business, can have Roth contributions up to that earned income. Money planted at fifteen gets fifty years of tax-free compounding, a runway no adult account will ever see again. Small numbers, absurd time horizons. If your teen earns a real paycheck, this is the conversation to have the same week.

Nobody told you the school decision is a cash flow decision wearing a values costume

Public, Montessori, private, parochial: families argue this as identity when they should first run it as math. Take the tuition, multiply by every year of the commitment, add the increases, and put that total next to your other goals, the retirement funding, the asset building, the house. There is no wrong answer here. There is only an unpriced one. A private school chosen with the full number on the table is a values decision. The same school chosen one fall at a time, refinanced around annually, is a slow-motion budget collapse with a crest on the blazer. Run all the years, then choose anything you want.

Nobody told you dependents change your return, or that your business can pay your kids

The credits attached to children are real money, they phase out at income levels worth knowing, and the household should adjust the W-4 in the birth year rather than discover the changes next April. And for the business owners: paying your child for legitimate work in the business, real tasks, real hours, reasonable wages, documented like any employee, is one of the cleanest family tax moves in the code, shifting income to a lower bracket and creating the earned income that unlocks the custodial Roth above. The whole move lives or dies on the word legitimate. Real work, real records. The version where a toddler is on payroll as a consultant is not a strategy, it is a Chapter 20 story with penalties.

And nobody told you the estate documents are part of having a baby

A will naming a guardian, life insurance sized to the actual job of replacing a parent's income for the years that matter, term insurance being the boring right answer for almost everyone, and beneficiaries updated on every account. This is the least fun paragraph in the chapter and the one that matters most. Parents who skip it are not risking money. They are delegating their child's future to a probate judge and a default formula. One afternoon, once, and it is done.

C.A.T. for Kids: Start at Five

Chapter 2 showed you that Q1 defaults get installed whether or not anyone installs them on purpose. Here is how to install them on purpose, and you can start as young as five, because the method shrinks to any size.

C, at kid size, is three jars: spend, save, give. Money arrives from small jobs and gifts, gets divided out loud, and a five year old learns the deepest lesson in this book before kindergarten ends: every dollar gets a job, and you are the one who assigns it. A, at kid size, is the save jar growing into the first asset conversation: the birthday money that opens a custodial investment account, the first statement read together at the kitchen table, a child watching money earn money and understanding, years before their peers, that dollars can work while you sleep. T, at kid size, can even be playful: some families take a small bite of every allowance as the household tax, and the child who grows up knowing a slice of every dollar belongs to the system will never be ambushed by a paycheck stub at twenty-two.

Then make it a table, not a lecture: a short family money meeting, weekly or monthly, where the jars get counted, the account gets checked, and the questions get answered honestly at whatever altitude the child can fly. The companion workbook has a C.A.T. for Kids exercise built for exactly this. You are your child's first CPA, and the tuition at this school is the cheapest it will ever be.

The C.A.T. Breakdown

C: The child is a permanent line in the truth layer, and the discipline is sequencing: rebuild the family budget before the birth, resize the reserve, automate the education funding at a sustainable number, and protect the gap, because the gap is now funding two futures. And enforce the oxygen mask rule without guilt: retirement funding before college funding, always, because your child can borrow for school and you cannot borrow for your sixties, and the greatest burden you can hand an adult child is a parent with no plan.

A: Run the account architecture deliberately: 529 for education, parent-owned. Custodial Roth the moment real earned income exists. Custodial UTMA only with full knowledge of the handover and the aid math. And understand the deeper A-move of this chapter: the child's Q1 is itself the asset you are building. A kid who watches parents run money as a calm system, who gets a custodial account as a teaching tool instead of a vault, who earns real money and sees it planted, inherits the operating system this whole book exists to install late in adults. You are not just funding a child. You are installing one.

T: The birth-year tax sequence: adjust the W-4, understand the credits and their phase-outs at your income, capture any state benefit on the 529 contributions, and, if a business exists, run the paying-your-kids analysis properly, with documentation, at legitimate wages. Every move in this paragraph is boring, written in black letter, and worth real money annually for eighteen consecutive years. Boring, repeated, compounds.

The Quarter Lens

Q1: This entire chapter is you, writing someone else's Q1, with full knowledge of what Q1 installs. The accounts matter. The atmosphere matters more. Both are now your job.

Q2: Most first children arrive here, into the exact decades when your own compounding matters most, which is why the oxygen mask rule and the automation matter so much: the Q2 parent is funding three futures at once, their own, the household's, and the child's, and only systems survive that math. Emotion alone does not.

Q3: The expensive childhood years, the school decisions at full price, the college cliff arriving on schedule. Q3 parents who planted in Q2 make these calls from a funded position. Q3 parents starting now still have moves, smaller runway, same method, and the honest conversation about what gets funded first.

Q4 and Overtime: The question inverts: how to help adult children without funding permanent dependence, how to gift with the tax rules instead of against them, and how the step-up and beneficiary decisions from Chapter 13 route what you built to the people you built it for. The parents who handle Q4 giving well are the ones who installed standards, not just accounts, back in Q1.

The Move to Make Now

Expecting, or planning to be: rebuild the family truth layer this month with the childcare line at real local prices, resize the reserve, and book the estate-document afternoon, will, guardian, term insurance, beneficiaries, before the due date.

Already a parent: open or verify the 529 this week and automate any sustainable number, because the calendar outranks the amount. Check every account title against the aid math and the handover rules. If a teenager earns real money, open the custodial Roth conversation this month. If a business exists, run the paying-your-kids analysis with your professional before year-end, documented properly.

Every parent, either way: run the full-years school math on whatever path you are on or considering, one page, all the years, next to your other goals. And write one sentence describing the money atmosphere your child currently absorbs, then decide if it is the one you mean to be installing.

The Warning

Two ditches, and love drives into both.

The first is guilt spending. The industry around children is engineered to convert love into invoices, and the Flexer has a parenting mode: the stroller as a status object, the birthday as a production, the school chosen for the sticker on the car. Your child cannot tell the difference between the expensive version and the present version of you. Everyone selling to you hopes you never notice that.

The second is martyrdom: parents who zero out their own futures in the child's name, no retirement funding, no assets, everything into the kid, and call it devotion. Run the movie forward: that math produces a fifty-year-old child financially carrying a seventy-five-year-old parent, which is the exact burden the devotion meant to prevent. Oxygen mask first. It is not selfish. It is sequencing, and your child is the beneficiary of it twice.

The Checklist

☐ Rebuild the family truth layer with real childcare and insurance numbers

☐ Resize the emergency reserve to the new household

☐ Complete the estate afternoon: will with guardian, term life insurance, all beneficiaries

☐ Open the 529, parent-owned, automated, this week

☐ Verify every account title against the handover and aid rules

The Before 40 Club Rule

Fund their future without unfunding yours. The account is a gift. The atmosphere is the inheritance.

One question before you go. What is my child absorbing about money from our house right now?

Put this chapter to work in the companion Before 40 Club Workbook at before40club.com.

CHAPTER 10:

BEFORE YOU START THE BUSINESS

"You do not get paid for potential. You get paid for execution."

The Expensive Lesson

Somewhere right now, a person is watching a video that tells them the secret to paying less tax is forming an LLC. Tomorrow they will pay a website a few hundred dollars, receive a certificate, and walk around with the warm feeling of having made a move. They have not made a move. They have bought a container. And a year from now they will be in an office like mine, confused about why nothing changed, holding a franchise tax bill from a state they do not live in, asking why the secret did not work.

Say the flag line again, because this is its home chapter: your LLC did not save you taxes. Your structure might.

A basic LLC, the single-member kind most people form, is what the IRS calls a disregarded entity, and disregarded is exactly the right word: for tax purposes, it is you, with no LLC, same return, same schedule, same self-employment tax, same everything. What an LLC gives you is legal separation, a real and valuable thing when maintained properly. What it does not give you is a single dollar of tax savings by itself. The savings, when they exist, come from what you run inside and on top of the container: the election, the salary, the books, the rhythm, the plan. The entity is the beginning of the sentence. The internet sold you the first word and told you it was the paragraph.

The expensive lesson of this chapter is bigger than the LLC myth, though. It is this: most people start businesses the way they buy houses, on emotion, at the ceiling, with the paperwork as an afterthought, and the paperwork is precisely the part that decides their taxes, their protection, and, if they ever build something big, their exit. The doing of the business is yours. The structure of the business is a discipline, and the discipline starts before the first dollar.

The Story

The parade through my office never stops. New owners arrive holding LLC certificates from a website, convinced the certificate itself is a business structure, a tax strategy, a force field. And the ones who worry me are not the confused ones, the confused ones ask questions. It is the confident ones, who have the container and nothing inside it: no separate business account, no business credit card, personal and company money swimming in one current. I have a term for it, financially disorganized, and it is the single most reliable predictor I know of a business that will not scale, because you might be the face of the company, but nobody can be the CFO of a shoebox.

Here is how the conversation actually goes at my desk, for my clientele of established owners: the LLC is the first basic element, the floor. The structure conversation gets genuinely interesting around the S election, and in my practice the sweet spot where that analysis starts paying for itself in earnest is roughly two hundred fifty thousand dollars in net profit, run against your real numbers, on paper, not against a video. Below the threshold, above it, either way the sequence never changes: clean accounts first, real books second, the election analysis annually, and the certificate framed on the wall where it belongs, as decoration.

Every one of those stories ends at the same sentence, so let me just hand it to you: the entity is a container. What you do inside it is the strategy. Most people stop at the container and wonder why nothing changed.

What Nobody Told You

Nobody told you what the entity menu actually is

In plain English: a sole proprietorship is you, doing business, no container, full personal exposure, simplest possible taxes. An LLC is a legal container that protects your personal assets from the business's problems, if you maintain the separation, while the taxes stay exactly yours. An S corporation is not an entity at all, it is a tax election, a set of rules you layer onto an LLC or corporation that can reduce self-employment tax at the right income level. And a C corporation is a separate taxpayer entirely, the structure of venture-backed companies and the doorway to QSBS, the exit provision from Chapter 15, and usually the wrong default for a small service business. That is the whole menu. Everything else is seasoning.

Nobody told you when the S election actually pays

Here is the honest math the videos skip. The S election lets an owner split what they take out of the business into two streams: a salary, which carries payroll taxes, and distributions, which do not. The savings live in that split. But the election also creates real costs: a payroll system, an additional tax return, more compliance, more accounting. Below a certain profit level, and for most service businesses that level is meaningfully higher than the internet implies, the costs eat the savings and the election is a net loss with extra paperwork. Above it, the election earns real money every year. The answer is not a rule of thumb from a video. It is a two-line analysis your professional runs against your actual profit, annually, because the right answer changes as the business grows. Elected too early is a common expensive mistake. Never analyzed is a more common one.

Nobody told you about the reasonable salary trap

The same videos that oversell the S election also whisper its abuse: pay yourself a tiny salary, take everything as distributions, keep all the payroll tax. The IRS has been watching that exact move for decades, the requirement is a reasonable salary for the work you actually do, and an S corporation owner taking large distributions on a token salary is one of the most well-lit audit profiles in the entire code. The strategy is the legitimate split at a defensible salary, documented. The fantasy version is not a strategy. It is a countdown, and you learned that word in Chapter 6.

Nobody told you that estimated taxes are not optional

The employee never sees this because the W-2 machine withholds invisibly. The owner is the machine now. Nothing is withheld from business income, the government expects its money quarterly, and underpaying as you go earns penalties even if you settle up in April. The infrastructure is Chapter 4's reserve wearing work clothes: a fixed percentage of every dollar of profit moves to the tax account on arrival, and four calendar dates a year, the reserve pays the estimates. Owners who run this rhythm find taxes boring. Owners who do not find them existential, every single year, on a schedule they somehow never see coming.

Nobody told you that mixing money dissolves everything

One checking account for the business, one for you, a clean transfer between them when you pay yourself, and no exceptions, ever. This is not accounting fussiness. It is load-bearing. Mixed money destroys your books, which destroys your deductions, which you learned in Chapter 6 are licensed by records. Mixed money turns tax time into archaeology at hourly rates. And mixed money can pierce the legal protection that was the entire point of the container: courts can disregard an LLC whose owner disregarded it first. The swipe of the business card at the grocery store costs three dollars of convenience and rents a crack in your whole structure.

And nobody told you to decide, on day one, what you are building

Two honest paths. A lifestyle business, built to fund your life at maximum take-home, wants simplicity: the LLC, the S analysis at the right profit, clean books, owner-sized retirement plans. A venture-scale company, built to take investment and exit, wants the C corporation from formation, a clean cap table, the 83(b) election filed inside its unforgiving window, and QSBS eligibility running from day one, because that exit clock, the one that can make millions of gain federally tax-free, starts at formation and cannot be backdated. Neither path is wrong. Choosing neither is. The founders who lose the most at exit lose it to decisions they did not know they were making in week one, and Chapter 15 holds the full accounting.

The C.A.T. Breakdown

C: A business is a second cash flow life, run parallel to your own, with its own truth layer: real revenue, real costs, real profit, and the owner's real take-home after the business keeps its own reserves. The discipline that separates businesses that survive from businesses that were exciting: the business holds its own emergency reserve, its own tax reserve fed automatically, and pays the owner a boring, regular amount, rather than the owner treating the business account as a personal ATM with a logo. Know your numbers well enough to answer fast. An owner who cannot state revenue, profit, and margin from memory is not running a business. The business is running them.

A: Here is the question that decides whether Chapter 5 recognizes your business as an asset: does it earn without your hours, or is it your job wearing a container? A practice where every dollar requires your personal presence is honorable work and it is still hour-renting, at a better rate, with more paperwork. The A-work of ownership is the slow conversion: documented processes, systems, people, anything that lets value reach a customer while you are elsewhere. Document your processes so the business is not just you. Every hour spent on that conversion is an hour spent manufacturing the only business that can ever be sold, and even if you never sell, it is the only kind you can ever take a vacation from.

T: The business unlocks the richest tax playbook a person can hold, and every page of it is licensed by the boring foundation: books that are current, records that survive questions, money that never mixed. On that foundation: the deductions for real business costs, the owner retirement plans with ceilings W-2 employees never see, the paying-your-kids move from Chapter 9, the entity election analyzed annually against real profit, the equipment expensing rules used because the business needed the equipment, never the reverse. Do not buy the truck for the write-off. And the year-end planning session from Chapter 6 stops being optional the day you own something, because the owner's calendar is where all of these moves live or die, and they all die on December 31.

The Quarter Lens

Q2: The launch quarter. Energy is highest, obligations are lightest, and a failure is a paid education instead of a catastrophe. It is also the myth quarter, where the container fantasy and the fake-guru tax advice do their damage on people too new to smell it. The Q2 owner's edge is doing the boring structure right at small scale, when mistakes are cheap and habits are forming: the separation, the reserve, the books, from dollar one.

Q3: The scale-or-coast quarter. Real profit makes every structural decision worth multiples: the S analysis at real numbers, the owner retirement plans finally fed at owner levels, the systems conversion turning the job into an asset. Q3 is also when the exit question becomes real for lifestyle businesses, and only the ones that became assets, systems, records, transferable operations, have anything to sell.

Q4: Transition. Sell, hand down, or wind down, and every path is priced by the earlier quarters: the clean books buyer diligence rewards, the structure the sale gets taxed through, the successor the systems made possible. Chapter 15's structural lessons and Chapter 13's family lessons meet here.

Overtime: A business with systems survives its founder. A business that was its founder is a job that ends, and the difference was decided decades earlier, in the A section of this chapter.

The Move to Make Now

Not yet started: write the one-page charter before any filing fee. What the business sells, to whom, the honest first-year revenue guess, and the path declaration, lifestyle or venture-scale, because that one word decides the structure. Then, and only then, form the container that matches, and open the business account the same week.

Already running: audit the foundation this month, five checks. Separation: is every dollar in a business account, and when did a personal swipe last happen? Reserve: does a fixed percentage of profit move to a tax account automatically, and are the four estimate dates on the calendar? Books: current within thirty days, or archaeology? Election: has anyone run the S analysis against this year's actual profit, in writing, dated? Numbers: can you state revenue, profit, and margin from memory right now?

Any check that fails is the assignment, in that order, because that is the order they collapse in.

The Warning

The internet is where business tax advice goes to become dangerous, and you will be marketed to relentlessly the moment the algorithms learn you own something. The tells are always the same: secrets the IRS hates, structures with too many boxes on the diagram, deductions that only work if nobody looks, and confidence perfectly uncorrelated with credentials. Run all of it through the Chapter 6 line: written rules, boring middle, real professional. The people selling the exotic version are monetizing your ownership, not participating in it, and they will not be seated beside you when the letter arrives.

And the warning underneath the warning: the container fantasy is really an agency fantasy, the hope that a document can do the work. It cannot. The certificate does not build the systems, keep the books, or make the calls. Nobody cares more than you will, no one is bigger than the program, and the program for owners is the least glamorous sentence in this book: separate the money, feed the reserve, keep the books, analyze the election, know the numbers. Owners who do that five-line program own businesses. Everyone else owns a certificate.

The Checklist

☐ Write the one-page charter, including the path declaration: lifestyle or venture-scale

☐ Match the container to the path before paying any filing fee

☐ Open the dedicated business account and end all mixing, permanently

☐ Automate the tax reserve percentage and calendar the four estimate dates

☐ Get books current within thirty days and keep them there

The Before 40 Club Rule

The entity is a container. The strategy is what you run inside it. Stop framing the certificate and start feeding the system.

One question before you go. Is my business a system, or is it me with a certificate on the wall?

Put this chapter to work in the companion Before 40 Club Workbook at before40club.com.

CHAPTER 11:

BEFORE YOU IGNORE THE IRS LETTER

"Release the bad energy and return to the objective."

The Expensive Lesson

There is an envelope in somebody's house right now, unopened, sitting under a stack of mail like a small radioactive object. The person who lives there knows exactly which envelope it is. They saw the return address. They put it down carefully, the way you put down something that might go off, and they have been managing their life around not opening it for eleven days.

I have spent 18 years on the other side of that envelope, and I can tell you the two facts that person needs more than anything. First: the letter is almost never as bad as the silence around it has become. Second: every single option they have is dying, one by one, in the order of most helpful first, while the envelope sits there. The IRS collection process is an escalator. It moves in one direction, on a published schedule, and it does not pause for your feelings about it. Standing still on an escalator is a decision.

The expensive lesson of this chapter comes in two halves, and both halves are behavior, not tax law. The worst thing you can do with an IRS letter is nothing. The second worst is panic and pay it blindly, because here is the fact that surprises everyone: the number on the notice is wrong far more often than people imagine. Not always, not even most of the time, but often enough that paying without checking is donating, and the IRS does not send thank-you cards. The letter is not the problem. Avoidance is the problem on one side, and blind panic is the problem on the other, and the entire chapter fits in the calm lane between them.

One more thing before the story, because it protects people: the IRS communicates by mail. Not by a threatening phone call demanding gift cards, not by text, not by a voicemail from a robot announcing your arrest. The scary call is a scam essentially every time. The boring envelope is the real one. The government's actual menace arrives with a barcode and terrible font choices.

The Story

A client came to me with the stack, the unopened IRS envelopes, and we did what I always do: sat down and opened them together, oldest first, because the oldest letter is where the story starts and it is always a smaller story than the fear says. That is the pattern this chapter is built on. The IRS has one institutional allergy, and it is being ignored. Ignore the letter and the machine concludes you are ignoring it, and the escalator does what escalators do.

But I want to tell you about the client who reversed the roles on me. When we totaled the file, the balance was close to two point two million dollars, and the shoulders that dropped in that meeting were mine, because the client was not bothered at all. Completely calm. And strangely, that calm was the most useful thing in the room, because calm people can execute. We built the package together, brought in the Taxpayer Advocate's office, and worked the balance down through the exact boring, procedural, deadline-respecting process this chapter teaches. Two point two million dollars, handled with paperwork and prudence. Whatever number is sitting in your drawer right now, I promise you it is smaller than that, and I promise you the process is the same: open it, read it, respond to it. The monster is a number. It was always a number.

The pattern under every version: the debt was never the emergency. The silence was. Balances have payment plans, disputes have procedures, and even the scary letters have rights attached with your name on them. Silence is the only move with no procedure and no rights, and it is the one people choose most, because fear does the choosing.

What Nobody Told You

Nobody told you the letters are a language, and the code in the corner is the whole sentence

Every real IRS notice carries a code, and the code tells you what this is, how serious it is, and what clock is running. Learn to read four of them and you can triage almost anything in your mailbox.

CP14 is the opener: the IRS believes you owe, here is the amount, here is the date. It is the beginning of a conversation, not a verdict, and handled promptly it is the cheapest letter in the sequence, the one where every option is still alive.

CP2000 is the mismatch letter, and hear this clearly: it is a proposal, not a bill. A computer compared what employers, banks, and brokers reported about you against what your return said, found a gap, and is proposing a change. The gap is frequently explainable and the proposed number is frequently wrong, a sale where the computer saw proceeds but not what you paid, income counted twice, a form that was corrected later. You have a written right to respond and disagree, with a deadline. People who read proposal as bill pay computers for their mistakes.

CP504 is the escalation: notice of intent to levy, the point where the tone changes and certain collection actions come into view. It is the letter this book's readers most often describe as the scary one, and the honest translation is: the polite phase is ending, the clock is now serious, and the window for the easy versions of every solution is closing. It is also still very solvable. What it is not, is ignorable.

LT11, and its sibling Letter 1058, is the final notice before levy, and it carries something the earlier letters do not: it triggers your legal right to a hearing, with a hard deadline to request it, a genuine procedural pause that exists specifically to protect you. Miss that window through avoidance and you did not just delay. You forfeited a right, and forfeited rights are the true cost of the unopened drawer.

Nobody told you the universal first move, so here it is, and it works on every letter ever sent

Four things, before you pay a dollar, call anyone, or lose a night of sleep. One: the tax year, because the letter is about a specific year, often not the one you assume, and everything downstream depends on it. Two: the actual amount, separated into tax, penalties, and interest, because those are different problems with different solutions. Three: the real deadline, printed on the notice, which defines exactly how much calm time you have, and there is almost always more than panic suggests. Four: whether the number is even correct, checked against your own return and records, because you now know how often it is not. Year, amount, deadline, accuracy. Every path, dispute, payment, plan, or professional help, starts from those four, and none of them can be found through the envelope.

Nobody told you what happens behind the silence

While the drawer stays closed, the machine proceeds: penalties accrue, interest compounds on the penalties, the notices escalate on schedule, refunds you were owed get intercepted and applied, and eventually the words levy and lien stop being vocabulary and start being logistics. None of that requires a human at the IRS to be angry at you. It is automation, and automation is the whole reason silence fails: you cannot wait out a machine. It has no lunch break and no memory of you either way.

And nobody told you when to handle it yourself versus getting help

The honest sorting: a small balance, clearly correct, on a year you understand, is a solvable errand, pay it or set up a payment plan directly, and the IRS's own systems for that are more workable than fear assumes. Get professional help when any of these is true: the amount is large relative to your life, the letter says levy or lien anywhere on it, the notice is wrong and the dispute is more than one document, multiple years are tangled together, a business or payroll is involved, or you have read the notice three times and still cannot say what it wants. The math on getting help is not complicated: options narrow as letters escalate, and a professional entering at CP14 is buying you choices that no longer exist by LT11. The most expensive representation is the kind hired last.

The C.A.T. Breakdown

C: An IRS balance is a cash flow event, and it should be run through Chapter 4 like any other: the real amount, the real deadline, and a payment approach your actual gap can carry, because a payment plan you default on is worse than a smaller one you keep. This is also where the tax reserve proves its whole existence: households running the Chapter 4 reserve read these letters as administration, because the money question was answered months ago. Households without it read the same letter as a crisis. Same envelope, different plumbing.

A: Ignored letters eventually reach for assets, liens that cloud the house, levies that reach accounts, and that is the real stake of this chapter for a builder: everything Chapter 5 plants grows inside a legal structure that assumes you answer your mail. Protecting the assets is not exotic. It is opening envelopes on time. And note the asymmetry that should motivate you: in the early letters, the IRS is flexible in ways that surprise people, plans, abatements, corrections. In the late letters, it is empowered in ways that surprise them more. Timing is the entire game, and you control timing exactly as long as you engage.

T: Prevention is upstream chapters doing their jobs: the reserve and estimates from Chapters 4 and 10 prevent the balance-due letters, the clean records from Chapter 6 win the mismatch letters, because a CP2000 dispute is exactly a records contest, and the professional relationship from Chapter 6 means the day a letter arrives, you already know who to hand it to. People with the system get fewer letters, and the letters they get are shorter conversations. The drawer people fund the difference.

The Quarter Lens

Q2: The first-letter quarter, usually born from side income without a reserve, a gig year without estimates, or a return done fast and cheap. The Q2 stakes are habit-setting: the person who handles their first notice calmly, four checks and a response, installs a default that protects them for life. The person who starts a drawer in Q2 is enrolling in a very long class.

Q3: The size quarter. Business income, equity events, and real money make Q3 notices bigger and more consequential, and the professional-help threshold from above is crossed almost by default. Q3 is also when old Q2 silence surfaces at compound interest, and the cleanup is measured in years.

Q4: Fixed incomes meet old balances, and collection against retirement-age taxpayers has its own hard realities. The kindest thing Q2-you and Q3-you can do for Q4-you is arrive there with zero open years and zero drawers.

Overtime: Estates inherit open tax problems, and executors, often your children, become the ones opening your drawer. Chapter 13 says it fully; this chapter says it plainly: do not bequeath an envelope.

The Move to Make Now

If there is an unopened letter in your life, this is the entire move: open it today, run the four checks, year, amount, deadline, accuracy, and write the four answers on the front of the envelope. That is it. That is the whole first step, and it will take eleven minutes, and the thing in your chest will be smaller at minute twelve than it has been in weeks. Then sort it honestly: solvable errand, or one of the get-help conditions, and act on the sort within one week.

If there is a drawer, multiple letters, months of silence, do not attempt archaeology alone and do not open them in random order. Gather everything, get professional eyes on the full stack at once, oldest first, because the sequence tells the story and the newest letter defines the live deadlines.

If your mailbox is clean: build the letter protocol now, in two lines, while nothing is at stake. Line one: any government letter gets opened the day it arrives and the four checks run. Line two: the name and number of who gets called if it is ever more than an errand. Households with a protocol never develop drawers, and the protocol costs nothing today.

The Warning

Two predators work this exact territory, and both hunt fear.

The first is the scammer: the call, the text, the voicemail threatening arrest, demanding immediate payment in gift cards or wire transfers, spoofing official numbers. The real IRS opens with letters, offers documented procedures, and never takes payment in gift cards, ever, under any circumstances. The scary call is theater. Hang up, and if doubt lingers, verify through official channels you look up yourself, never through numbers the caller provides.

The second predator is legal and on the radio: the settle-for-pennies industry, the firms that monetize panic with enormous promises, enormous upfront fees, and outcomes their fine print never guaranteed. Real relief programs exist, real professionals use them, and the honest ones will tell you whether you qualify before taking serious money, because qualification is checkable. The tell is the same as every fraud in this book: manufactured urgency, guaranteed outcomes, and pressure to pay before anyone has read your actual file. The Avoider from Chapter 20 is these firms' entire business model. Do not be the inventory.

The Checklist

☐ Open any unopened government letter today, no exceptions

☐ Run the four checks: tax year, amount, deadline, accuracy against your records

☐ Identify the code and what stage of the escalator it represents

☐ Sort honestly: solvable errand or get-help condition, and act within one week

☐ If a hearing-rights letter (LT11/1058): calendar the request deadline immediately

The Before 40 Club Rule

The letter is a number wearing a costume. Open it, read the code, run the four checks, and take the costume off.

One question before you go. What envelope, literal or digital, am I not opening?

Agency: The envelope is openable, the deadline is readable, the response is writable. Which is yours to do first? **Urgency:** What response date goes on the calendar today, before the escalator moves?

Put this chapter to work in the companion Before 40 Club Workbook at before40club.com.

CHAPTER 12:

THE HIGH EARNER TRAP

"A large income without ownership is still fragile."

The Expensive Lesson

There is a person in your city right now making $400,000 a year who cannot survive four months without a paycheck. They have the house, the cars, the schools, the trips, the watch, and a net worth that would embarrass their income if the two were ever introduced. They are not lying to anyone on purpose. They are just living inside the most sophisticated trap in personal finance, the one nobody warns you about because from the outside it looks exactly like winning.

I have read these returns for 18 years, and here is the sentence I need engraved somewhere you will see it daily: high income does not mean wealth. Income is a rate. Wealth is a stock. Income is water flowing through a pipe. Wealth is water that stayed. The trap works because everyone, the earner included, keeps confusing the flow for the level, and the entire economy around a high earner is engineered to keep the confusion running: the lenders who approve more, the neighborhoods that expect more, the peers who spend more, the very identity of being someone who has made it, which turns out to be an expensive costume with a monthly bill.

The expensive lesson, and it is the line from Chapter 4 arriving at full volume: income exposes your system. It does not fix it. A broken system at $80,000 is stress. A broken system at $400,000 is stress with better scenery, higher stakes, more embarrassment blocking the fix, and a tax profile that punishes the disorganization harder every year. More money poured into a leaking bucket does not repair the bucket. It just makes a more impressive puddle, and it delays the day you look down, which is the most expensive delay of your life, because Q2 and Q3 compounding does not wait for your awakening.

This chapter is the honest audit for the people the other chapters supposedly do not apply to. It applies to you hardest.

The Story

I had a client with an elite W-2 who bought a G-Wagon. The feed was Mykonos, Dubai, five-star restaurants, and if you scrolled it you would have ranked him among the winners. I did not have to scroll. I had the return and the statements, and they told the other story: credit cards likely maxed, asset schedules nearly empty, the entire financial life performing an income instead of keeping one. That is the return that looks like two different people, and in New York I have seen more of them than I can count, because a high-income city is a machine for confusing the flow with the level.

Here is what I asked him, and what I am asking you: the W-2 is strong today, but what does Q3 of your life look like? What about Q4? What about the season with elderly parents? Keeping up with the Joneses is the most expensive sport in America because looking the part and being the part are two different careers, and only one of them compounds. Being the part is inside work, quiet work, the gap, the assets, the plan, and it produces nothing to post. You have a short window on this earth. Spend it becoming the thing, not performing it.

The detail that repeats across every version of that story: the high earner always thought they had a tax problem. They never had a tax problem. They had a system problem with a tax symptom, and treating the symptom, chasing deductions, resenting brackets, buying things for write-offs, only fed the disease. The system is this chapter.

What Nobody Told You

Nobody told you that lifestyle creep is not a character flaw, it is a default setting

Every raise arrives with a matching invitation: the housing that fits the new income, the car that matches the parking lot, the vacations your new peers consider normal. Chapter 2 taught you that normal is the most expensive word you own, and high income buys admission to progressively more expensive normals, each one presented as simply what people like you do. Nobody decides to inflate their lifestyle. They just never decide not to, and the default does the rest. The fix is mechanical, not moral, and you already have it: the raise capture rule from Chapter 4, half of every increase to the gap, automated before the new money ever touches the checking account, forever. High earners who run that one rule become wealthy almost accidentally. High earners who do not become expensive.

Nobody told you about the golden handcuffs

Here is the trap inside the trap: the inflated lifestyle does not just consume the income, it takes the income hostage. Once the fixed costs are built for the big salary, the big salary becomes mandatory, and mandatory income is the death of options. You cannot take the risk, start the thing, change the field, call the bluff, or walk away from the room where you are disrespected, because the mortgage has a vote now, and the school has a vote, and the lease has a vote. The person earning $150,000 with a fat gap has more real freedom than the person earning $500,000 at breakeven, and freedom was supposedly the point. The handcuffs are gold, and they are still handcuffs, and you installed them one upgrade at a time.

Nobody told you that one W-2 is concentration risk wearing a suit

The high earner's entire empire usually stands on a single payer: one employer, one industry, one set of hours, one health. Chapter 5 called this a diagnosis and here is the full chart: your income can be terminated in a meeting you are not invited to, your industry can reprice in a cycle, and your hours have the ceiling your body sets. High earners feel diversified because the number is big. A big number from one source is not diversification. It is a large single point of failure, and the entire A chapter of this book is the treatment: convert flow into stock, income into assets, while the flow is at its peak, because peak flow is precisely the moment conversion is cheapest and precisely the moment nobody feels the urgency to do it.

Nobody told you how your bonus and equity are actually taxed, so every year you feel robbed on schedule

The bonus arrives visibly smaller than announced, and the group chat declares bonuses are taxed higher. They are not. Bonuses are withheld at a flat supplemental rate up front, which can be more or less than your real rate, and the truth settles at filing. The problem is not a special bonus tax. The problem is planning your life around the gross announcement instead of the net reality, and letting a withholding estimate ambush your cash flow. Equity compensation is the same story with higher stakes: shares that vest are generally income at vesting whether or not you sell, and the high earner who holds everything, concentrated in the same employer that already owns their paycheck, has doubled the single point of failure and called it loyalty. The moves are boring and known: know the net before you spend the gross, know the tax event before it lands, and treat vested equity as money that must justify staying concentrated, not money that needs a reason to diversify.

And nobody told you the brackets are not the enemy, the disorganization is

High earners love to narrate their tax bill as persecution, and the narration is expensive because it points at the unfixable and away from the fixable. You cannot vote your bracket down tonight. You can, tonight, be the person from Chapter 6 whose accounts are maxed, whose timing is planned, whose entity, if a business exists, is analyzed, whose effective rate is known by heart and bending year over year. In 18 years I have never met a high earner with a full system who felt persecuted. I have met hundreds without one who did, and their returns showed the same signature: maximum income, maximum default settings, zero planning, and a bill that was mostly a disorganization invoice with the government's name on it.

Nobody told you about health debt

There is a version of the trap that never appears on a statement. Some high earners look successful because they are borrowing, not from a bank, but from sleep, from physical health, from mental health, from relationships, and from future energy, and that loan compounds like every other one. Here is the sentence to test your own situation against: your income is overstated if maintaining it requires you to continually borrow against your health. The elite W-2 funded by four hours of sleep and a skipped decade of physicals is not a high income, it is a high income minus an unbooked liability, and the balloon payment on health debt arrives in Q3 and Q4 with interest. The keep rate this chapter taught you has a physical twin: what did the year take out of the machine, and what did you put back?

The C.A.T. Breakdown

C: The high earner's truth layer has one extra line and one extra rule. The extra line: net-of-everything income, after taxes, after the fixed lifestyle, the number that shows how much of the mighty flow actually survives each month, because that survivor number, not the salary, is your real financial capacity, and for most unaudited high earners it is humiliatingly small. The extra rule: every fixed cost is a hostage-taker, so the audit question on each one is not can we afford this but what does this cost us in options. Run the Chapter 8 stress test on the whole life, not just the house: three months of no income, what survives? A high earner who cannot answer calmly has a high salary and no position.

A: Peak income is a conversion window, not a lifestyle license, and the window is narrower than it feels because it is bounded by career risk on one side and compounding math on the other. The assignment is Chapter 5 at maximum aggression: automate conversion at a percentage that almost hurts, build the position outside the employer, diversify vested equity on a written rule instead of a feeling, and measure yourself monthly on the only scoreboard that matters here: what fraction of my lifetime earnings have I kept? Flow is what you rent. Stock is what you own. Convert while the converting is good.

T: The high earner's tax playbook is mostly Chapter 6 executed without excuses, because every move is worth more at your rates: the accounts maxed first, all of them, before any exotic conversation, the timing of income and gains planned across years instead of endured, the withholding on bonuses and equity reconciled to reality instead of discovered in April, the charitable giving structured instead of scattered if giving is real for you, and the mid-year planning rhythm that is optional at $80,000 and negligent to skip at $400,000. And one hard rule for this income class specifically: no strategy whose primary feature is that it sounds unavailable to ordinary people. Your rates make you the favorite target of every scheme seller in the country. The boring middle is where your money is. The exotic edge is where it goes to be featured in Chapter 20.

The Quarter Lens

Q2: The trap is set here. The first big salary arrives, the lifestyle calibrates to it, and the defaults harden while the earner is too busy earning to notice. A Q2 high earner who installs the capture rule and the conversion machine before the lifestyle calcifies is playing the game on the easiest setting it will ever offer. Every year of delay raises the difficulty.

Q3: The trap either springs or pays. Peak earnings meet either a conversion machine, and the numbers get genuinely large, or a peak lifestyle, and the golden handcuffs lock at maximum weight exactly as career risk peaks, the age premium in hiring turns against you, and the recovery runway shortens. Q3 is also when the one-payer risk stops being theoretical for many people, and the difference between the two Q3s is nothing but Q2 behavior.

Q4: The verdict quarter. Flow stops for everyone eventually, and Q4 asks one question: how much of it stayed? The high earner with converted assets barely notices the transition. The high earner without them discovers, at the worst possible time, that they were never wealthy, only well paid, and the distinction arrives with no grace period.

Overtime: Only stock transfers. Nobody inherits a salary. The flow dies with the job, and everything Chapter 13 and the Overtime close discuss presumes there is stock to steward. Peak flow, converted, is the entire estate. Peak flow, consumed, is a eulogy full of trips.

The Move to Make Now

The audit, this week, four numbers on one page. One: real monthly take-home, the Chapter 4 number, at your actual withholding. Two: real fixed monthly cost, everything contractual and everything functionally contractual, the school, the lease, the life.

Three: the survivor number, one minus two, which is your true capacity and probably a shock. Four: the keep rate, your net worth excluding home equity divided by your rough total lifetime earnings, a percentage that answers the only question: of all the water that flowed, how much stayed?

Then three installations within thirty days. The capture rule, automated on the next raise or bonus, half to the gap before it lands. The conversion machine, a fixed monthly percentage into assets, at a level that competes with the lifestyle instead of losing to it. And the equity rule if equity exists: a written diversification policy, executed on vesting dates by calendar instead of by mood.

And one subtraction: identify the single fixed cost that costs the most freedom per dollar, the hostage-taker in chief, and begin its removal this quarter. Not the latte. The lease, the second car, the membership performing an identity. High earners do not need a thousand cuts. They need one hostage released at a time.

The Warning

The resistance to this chapter will not feel like resistance. It will feel like reasonable objections, and they will arrive in your own voice: I work hard, I deserve this. Everyone at my level lives this way. I will get serious after the next bonus, the next promotion, the vest date. It is fine, the income is not going anywhere. Read that last one again slowly, because every corner office I have ever watched empty out believed it on a Tuesday.

And the deeper warning: the Flexer from Chapter 20 does his most expensive work in this income class, because here he can afford real damage. Performing wealth on a high income is the most convincing performance there is, convincing enough to fool the performer, and the audience it plays for, the neighbors, the feed, the strangers at red lights, is not going to fund your Q4. Looking rich and being free sit at opposite ends of the same paycheck, and every month, your allocations vote for one of them. Nobody cares more than you will, and no one is bigger than the program, especially not the well paid.

The Checklist

☐ Compute the four numbers: take-home, fixed cost, survivor number, keep rate

☐ Automate the capture rule: half of every raise and bonus to the gap, permanently

☐ Set the conversion machine: fixed monthly percentage to assets, at a level that competes

☐ Write the equity diversification rule and calendar it to vesting dates

☐ Reconcile bonus and equity withholding against your real rate before spending any gross number

The Before 40 Club Rule

Income is the flow. Wealth is what stayed. You are not what you make. You are what you kept.

One question before you go. If my income stopped today, how many months would my lifestyle survive?

Agency: The capture rule, the stress test, the hostage-taking fixed cost: which lever is yours to pull? **Urgency:** Which bonus or raise gets captured before the lifestyle finds it, and by what date?

Put this chapter to work in the companion Before 40 Club Workbook at before40club.com.

CHAPTER 13:

BEFORE YOU HELP FAMILY WITH MONEY

"Right-size relationships."

The Expensive Lesson

The most dangerous financial requests you will ever receive will come from people you love, and they will arrive at the exact moments you are least equipped to evaluate them: the emergency call, the wedding season, the business idea at the cookout, the parent aging faster than anyone admitted, the sibling between things again. Family money is the category where smart people make their worst decisions, because every safeguard this book installs, the truth layer, the boring questions, the written rules, feels like betrayal when the counterparty shares your last name.

Let me say the hard sentence early so the chapter can be useful: your friends do not need access to your money to cost you money, and neither does your family, and family has better access. Family knows your numbers, or thinks it does. Family holds history as collateral. Family can invoice you in guilt, a currency with no exchange rate and no receipts. None of that makes family the enemy. It makes family the highest-stakes counterparty you will ever face, which means family money deserves more structure, not less, and almost everyone runs it with none at all.

And the second hard sentence, the one about the other direction: the largest family money event of your life is probably not a loan you make. It is the aging and eventual loss of your parents, and it is the event families prepare for least, because preparing feels like inviting it. It is not about the paperwork, until the paperwork blindsides the whole family, at the worst week of their lives, with the lawyers billing hourly. This chapter covers both directions, the money flowing down and sideways to family, and the money and responsibility flowing toward you as parents age, and the core discipline is identical: structure, decided early, while everyone is healthy and nobody is emotional. Love is the reason for the structure. It was never the substitute for it.

The Story

Here is my operating doctrine on family money, built from watching it go wrong in every direction. First rule: any money you hand to family, expect never to get it back. Price it as a gift in your heart no matter what it is called out loud, and if it must be a loan, put a promissory note on paper, not because you will sue your cousin but because paper keeps the memory honest on both sides. Second rule, and this one took me years: transparency beats capacity. You are allowed to say, I do not have it right now, and you are allowed to ask, do you have any assets you could sell first? Those two sentences feel impossible the first time and they are the most loving structural move in this chapter, because here is what I have learned: if you keep giving and giving, people will keep asking and asking. The generosity trains the requests.

The deeper reason I do not recommend lending to family and friends at all is the emotions. Money between loved ones gets tangled with ethics, values, morals, and loyalty, four things that never appear on a balance sheet and always appear in the argument. So the structure exists to protect the relationship, not the dollars: a stated capacity, a named category for every dollar that moves, and the honesty to say the true number out loud, including when the true number is zero.

Both directions teach the same lesson from opposite ends: the conversations feel unbearable to start and trivial in hindsight, and the silence feels comfortable in the moment and catastrophic at the end. Every family is one honest meeting away from a completely different outcome, and almost no family holds the meeting.

What Nobody Told You

Nobody told you the difference between a gift, a loan, and a subsidy, and the confusion is the damage

A gift is money that leaves with no expectation of return, decided in advance, sized to what you can lose without resentment. A loan is money with written terms, a schedule, and consequences, exactly like the bank version, because the paper is what keeps the relationship clean. A subsidy is what most family money actually becomes: an undefined, recurring, resented flow that everyone calls a loan and nobody treats as one. The rule that saves relationships: decide which of the three it is before the money moves, say it out loud, and if it is a loan, write it down, amount, schedule, what happens on a miss. If writing it down feels like it would insult them, you already know it is not a loan. It is a gift wearing a costume, so either give the gift openly and smaller, or decline. The unspoken loan is how families lose the money and each other, and it never had to be a choice between the two.

Nobody told you that your ability to help is an asset that requires protection

The Chapter 4 rule applies with family force: help comes from the gap, never from the reserve, never from the retirement funding, never from debt taken in your name for someone else's life, and co-signing is debt in your name with someone else's behavior attached, which is the worst instrument in consumer finance. Set your family help capacity as a real number, annually, in advance, the amount you can deploy without endangering your own program, because the parent who torches their Q4 to fund an adult child's Q2 has not helped twice, they have created two crises on a delay. The oxygen mask rule from Chapter 9 governs the whole extended family: secured people can help for decades. Depleted people can help once, badly.

Nobody told you that the parent conversation is a checklist, not a confrontation

While your parents are living and well is the entire window, and the agenda is shorter than the dread suggests. Where the documents live: the will, any trust, the deed, the policies, the account list, findable by the people who will need them. Whether the two documents that govern a crisis exist: the power of attorney for finances and the healthcare directives, because without them, a stroke does not just take a parent's health, it freezes their accounts behind a court process while the bills continue. Whether the beneficiary designations match reality, because Chapter 7 taught you the form outranks the will, and a parent's retirement account naming a deceased spouse or an estranged ex is a common, silent, total misdirection of everything. And who is expected to do what, said out loud, while everyone can hear it, because the siblings who divide roles at a kitchen table stay siblings, and the ones who divide them at a funeral often do not.

Nobody told you that gifting now versus inheriting later is a real tax fork, and picking blind costs six figures

Here is the plain-English version of the biggest concept in this chapter: the step-up in basis. When you inherit an appreciated asset, the house, the stock, its cost basis generally resets to its value at death, which can erase decades of taxable gain, entirely, legally, by default. When you receive the same asset as a lifetime gift, you generally receive the old basis too, and the embedded tax bill with it. That single rule means the loving instinct, put the house in the kids' names now, is frequently the most expensive move available, forfeiting the reset and sometimes creating exposure and aid complications nobody priced. Sometimes lifetime gifting is right, the annual exclusion amounts, funding the grandchildren's 529s from Chapter 9, and larger strategies at real estates. The point is the fork is real, the default answers are usually wrong, and this is precisely the decision that needs the CPA and the estate attorney in the same conversation, before anything moves, while everyone is alive to choose.

Nobody told you what the executor actually signs up for, or what inherited accounts demand

When a parent dies, someone, often you, becomes the estate's project manager with legal duties attached: the final individual return still has to be filed for the year of death, the estate itself may need its own return if it earns income while settling, the assets must be found, valued, protected, and distributed by the rules, and the executor is personally on the hook for doing it in the right order. Inherited retirement accounts carry their own clocks, most non-spouse beneficiaries now must empty inherited accounts within a decade, a compressed schedule with real tax planning inside it, and an inherited home sold without understanding the step-up can hand the IRS money the law never asked for. None of this is unmanageable. All of it is brutal to learn for the first time in grief, which is why the checklist above, done early, is the actual gift.

And nobody told you that boundaries are a form of generosity

The family member who funds everything teaches everyone to bring requests. The one with clear, calm, consistent rules, this is what I do, this is what I do not do, this is the number, teaches everyone to bring plans. Chapter 20 named the Loyalist, the goofball face that cannot say no, so his money says yes for him, and the Loyalist's tragedy is that his boundlessness helps no one: the recipients stay dependent, the resentment compounds silently, and the day his capacity finally breaks, everyone falls at once. The most generous people I know in real life are structured about it, and the structure is why they are still generous at seventy.

The C.A.T. Breakdown

C: Family help is a budget line, not an emergency response. Set the annual capacity number from the gap, hold the reserve sacred, and when the request exceeds the number, the answer is the number, offered cleanly, not the reserve offered resentfully. And run the truth layer on any recurring support honestly: a monthly subsidy to an adult child or a sibling is a fixed cost from Chapter 12, a hostage-taker, and it deserves the same audit as the lease, including the question no one asks: is this money building their system or replacing their need for one?

A: Two asset disciplines. Downstream: never convert your assets into family liquidity under pressure, no cashing retirement accounts for someone's emergency, no home equity for someone's venture, no co-signed instruments, because Chapter 5 built that position across decades and a single emotional weekend can unwind it. Upstream: the parents' assets need a map before they need a manager, the account list, the titles, the deed, the policies, findable, because unfound assets are the estate's silent leak, and the step-up decision from above is, dollar for dollar, one of the largest single asset moves your family will ever make or miss.

T: The family tax playbook, boring and black-letter as always: the annual gift exclusion used deliberately instead of accidentally, the 529 funding as the cleanest grandparent gift, the step-up preserved unless a professional analysis says otherwise, the beneficiary forms audited every few years because they outrank the will, the final and estate returns understood before the executor role lands, and the ten-year clock on inherited accounts planned across brackets instead of ignored until year nine. Every item on that list is decided well in a calm year and badly in a grieving one, and the calendar is the only thing that chooses which year you get.

The Quarter Lens

Q2: The squeeze begins here for many: the first real income arrives, and with it the requests, at exactly the moment your own compounding matters most. The Q2 discipline is installing the structure before the pattern sets, the capacity number, the gift-loan-subsidy rule, the boundaries, because the precedent you set at thirty is the expectation you service at fifty.

Q3: The sandwich quarter, and this chapter's center of gravity: children still climbing, parents beginning to descend, and you at peak earnings, which the whole family can see. Q3 is when the parent checklist stops being theoretical, when the executor role approaches, and when the households that did this chapter early operate on a plan while the others improvise in hospital hallways.

Q4: You switch sides of every conversation in this chapter. The documents are now yours to have ready, the map is yours to draw, the kitchen-table meeting is yours to call, and the discipline of helping adult children without funding dependence becomes the daily test. The best Q4 gift to your family is the one your parents may or may not have given you: being organized, early, out loud.

Overtime: The chapter's final exam. Everything transfers, cleanly by design or expensively by default, and the difference was never wealth. Families of modest means transfer smoothly on structure, and wealthy families detonate on silence, every year, in every probate court in the country. Legacy is not the amount. Legacy is the amount times the organization.

The Move to Make Now

Three moves, staged over ninety days.

First, this week, alone: set your numbers and rules in writing. The annual family help capacity. The gift-loan-subsidy decision rule. The two personal statutes: no co-signing, and no help from the reserve or retirement, ever. Written rules, decided calm, are what you will quote to yourself under pressure, and under pressure is the only time they matter.

Second, this month, the parent conversation, if your parents are living: frame it as organization, not mortality. One meeting, the checklist above, documents located, POA and healthcare directives confirmed or scheduled, beneficiaries verified, roles said out loud. If it helps, blame this book. I volunteer.

Third, this quarter, your own side: your will, your beneficiaries, your document map, findable by the person who would need them, because Chapter 9 assigned this to parents and this chapter assigns it to everyone. You are someone's kitchen-table conversation too.

And if a live request is sitting in front of you right now: run it through the rule before you respond. Gift, loan, or subsidy. Capacity or beyond it. If loan, paper, or it is a gift, resized. Answer within a week, cleanly, whatever the answer is. Slow clean answers preserve families. Fast murky ones bill them for years.

The Warning

Two failure modes, and they wear each other's clothes.

The first is the wall: reading this chapter as permission to become the family's least reachable member, hoarding behind boundaries, letting structure do the work of coldness. That is not the program. Family is one of the reasons for the program, and a capacity number of zero, at real income, is not discipline, it is the Flexer's cousin, hoarding as identity. The structure exists so you can help sustainably for fifty years, not so you can decline elegantly for fifty years.

The second is the sponge: the Loyalist, absorbing every request, mistaking depletion for devotion, teaching the whole system that planning is unnecessary because you exist. Watch his trajectory: beloved at thirty-five, quietly resented and resenting at fifty, and a crisis to the very family he carried by sixty-five, because nobody caught him and he never asked. A misaligned person is an expensive liability, and a boundaryless one is an expensive certainty, even when, especially when, the misalignment is generosity with no operating system.

The lane between the wall and the sponge is narrow, and it is drawn with the three tools of this chapter: a number, a rule, and a conversation held early. Purpose comes first, and the purpose of family money is a family that still likes each other in Overtime.

The Checklist

☐ Set the annual family help capacity number, in writing

☐ Adopt the gift-loan-subsidy rule: named out loud before money moves, loans on paper or resized to gifts

☐ Enact the two statutes: no co-signing, no help from reserve or retirement

☐ Hold the parent meeting: document locations, POA, healthcare directives, roles out loud

☐ Audit beneficiary designations, yours and, where possible, your parents', against current reality

The Before 40 Club Rule

Structure is not the opposite of love. Structure is how love survives money. Decide everything early, out loud, on paper.

One question before you go. What is my honest annual family help capacity, decided calmly, in advance?

Agency: Your capacity number and your rules are entirely yours to set. Have you set them? **Urgency:** Which pending family conversation gets its honest answer this week?

Put this chapter to work in the companion Before 40 Club Workbook at before40club.com.

CHAPTER 14:

BEFORE YOU BUY THE RENTAL

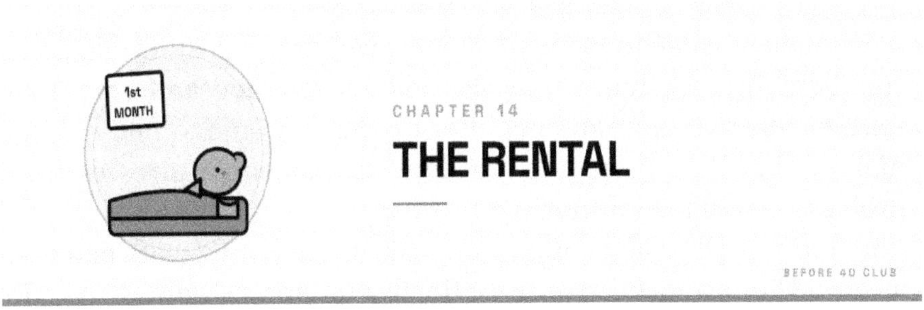

The Expensive Lesson

Real estate is where the asset chapter of this book gets its most famous graduates and its most preventable casualties, and the difference between the two groups is visible before the closing, every single time.

The graduates bought math. The casualties bought a story.

The story version goes like this, and you have heard it at a barbecue: real estate always goes up, tenants pay your mortgage, it is passive income, my cousin has four doors and quit his job. The story is not entirely false, and that is what makes it dangerous, because the true parts, the leverage, the tax treatment, the tenant paying principal, only pay the people who bought the property the boring way: at a real number, with real reserves, after the honest spreadsheet, with the tax playbook read in advance. Everyone else bought the fantasy monthly cash flow from the listing, met the actual one in February when the boiler died into a vacancy, and discovered that a rental is not passive income. A rental is a small business with a roof, and Chapter 10 applies to it in full: it needs its own truth layer, its own reserves, its own records, and an owner who knows the numbers cold.

The expensive lesson: real estate is the asset family with the best tax playbook in the entire code and the least forgiveness for emotional buyers. The code will hand you depreciation, exchanges, and step-ups. The market will hand you nothing for feelings. Buy the spreadsheet, and the property comes with it. Buy the property, and the spreadsheet arrives later, as an invoice.

The Story

A client came to me with about seven properties in Ohio and a confident forecast: Busayo, we should clear ten thousand a month in rent, maybe five thousand net after expenses. Come to find out, the man was in a hole. Properties that could not be rented, an assessment problem tied to the location, and a financial advisor who had steered him into a bad deal and gotten paid to do it. The listing math had been a story. The spreadsheet, once we finally built it, was a different genre entirely.

And then there is the phone call this chapter is named for. A client sold a property and called me sixty days later, after the closing, asking about options. The 1031 conversation, the qualified intermediary, the clocks, all of it has to exist before the sale, and none of it can be conjured afterward, so what he had instead was a six-figure tax bill that one earlier phone call would have deferred. So here is the whole discipline in one sentence: be the boring buyer. Underwrite the real after-tax cash flow, talk to your CPA before you buy and before you sell, understand cost segregation and the 1031 rules while they can still help you, and run your life off the model, not the fantasy. The fantasy is free right up until it invoices you.

The pattern under the casualty stories is always the same and always cheap to fix: the information was public, the rules were written, and the phone call was available, before the purchase, before the sale, before the deadline. Real estate does not punish ignorance with a warning. It punishes it with a wire transfer. This chapter is the phone call, in advance.

What Nobody Told You

Nobody told you the real spreadsheet, so here it is

The honest monthly math on any rental: real rent, at the number comparable units actually lease for, not the listing's optimism, minus a vacancy factor, because every unit sits empty sometimes and pretending otherwise is the first lie, minus the mortgage, taxes at the reassessed rate, and insurance, minus a maintenance percentage, the

Chapter 8 reality that buildings age in silence, minus a capital reserve line for the roof, the boiler, the systems with known lifespans and known prices, minus management, either the fee you pay or the honest value of your own hours, because Chapter 5 taught you that an asset earning your hours back is partly a job. What remains after every line is the real cash flow, and the discipline is brutal and simple: if the real number is negative, you are not buying an investment, you are buying a monthly bill with a story attached, and appreciation is a hope, not a line item. Buy properties whose spreadsheets work today. Hope is not a strategy; it is the thing casualties were holding.

Nobody told you that depreciation is the quiet superpower of the whole asset class

In plain English: the tax code lets you deduct a slice of the building's cost every year, on paper, while the property may be appreciating in reality. That paper loss can shelter the rental's real cash flow from tax, which is why a property can put money in your pocket monthly and show little or no taxable income, entirely by design, entirely in the written rules. This is the single biggest reason Chapter 5 called real estate the family with the most tax advantages attached. Two footnotes belong in the same breath. First, depreciation is not optional in spirit: skip claiming it and the code generally treats you as if you had claimed it anyway when you sell, the worst of both worlds. Second, the bill returns at the exit, which is the next paragraph, and knowing both halves before you buy is the difference between a strategy and a surprise.

Nobody told you about recapture, the tax bill people forget they are building

All those years of depreciation deductions lowered your basis, and when you sell, the government collects its deferred share: the depreciation you took gets recaptured and taxed, at rates worth knowing in advance, on top of the capital gain. None of this makes depreciation a bad deal; deferral plus the time value of money is a genuinely good trade. But sellers who never heard the word recapture meet it at closing as an ambush, and ambushes, as this entire book keeps saying, are just planning that never happened. Price the exit when you model the entrance.

Nobody told you the 1031 exchange rules before they sold, and that sentence has cost people millions

Here is the move in plain English: when you sell an investment property, the code lets you roll the entire gain into the next investment property and defer the tax, keeping every dollar working instead of sending a slice to Washington between deals. It is the compounding engine behind most large real estate portfolios. And here is why it belongs in the before chapter: the structure must exist before you close the sale. The money cannot touch your hands, a qualified intermediary must hold it, and two clocks start the day you close: forty-five days to formally identify the replacement property, one hundred eighty days to close on it, and the calendar does not negotiate, extend for weekends, or care about your reasons. Sellers who call after closing are calling about a tax bill, not an exchange. Sellers who call sixty days before are calling about a strategy. Same property, same gain, same code. The phone call's date is the entire difference.

Nobody told you the supporting playbook, so here is the tour

Cost segregation: an engineering-based study that splits a property into components that depreciate faster, front-loading the paper losses into the early years when they are worth most, a real tool at real price points, worth a professional conversation on larger purchases rather than a guess. Real estate professional status: a specific set of tests that, for people who genuinely work in real estate at qualifying hours, changes how rental losses can offset other income, powerful, heavily documented, heavily scrutinized, and absolutely not a checkbox for people with day jobs, whatever the internet says. The primary-residence conversions in both directions: living in a former rental, or renting a former home, each carries its own rules about the exclusion from Chapter 8 and the basis math, and each is a planned move, not an improvised one. And the ending Chapter 13 already taught you: hold an appreciated property to death and the step-up can erase the embedded gain for your heirs entirely, which is why die with it is, unromantically, a legitimate line item in real estate exit planning, and why the sell-exchange-or-hold decision late in life belongs in the same room as your estate documents.

And nobody told you how to hold it

The entity question from Chapter 8 returns with a different answer: for investment property, the liability logic that was overkill on your own home becomes real, a tenant's lawsuit should meet a structure, not your personal balance sheet. The standard shape is the LLC per property or small cluster, with the Chapter 10 disciplines in force, separate money, real books, maintained formalities, because a pierced entity from mixed funds protects nothing. The footnotes that trip people: financing often complicates entity ownership, insurance is the first line of defense regardless of structure, and umbrella coverage is the cheap, boring layer almost every landlord should price. Decide the structure before the offer, with professional eyes, because retitling later is friction and sometimes triggers consequences the day-one decision avoids for free.

The C.A.T. Breakdown

C: Every property is its own truth layer, run monthly like the business it is: the real spreadsheet above, reserves funded from rent before profit is declared, and the portfolio-level view once doors multiply, because two properties can hide one loser in a blended number. The Chapter 4 rule wears a landlord's clothes here: a rental without its own reserve account is a personal emergency scheduled in advance, and the boiler knows your reserve balance. It always knows.

A: Real estate is Chapter 5 with leverage, and leverage cuts both ways with total indifference. The tenant pays down principal while the asset appreciates, equity building from two directions at once, which is the legitimate magic. The same borrowing magnifies every mistake: overpaying, under-reserving, fantasy rents. The A discipline is buying on the number, sizing debt so the property survives vacancies and rate reality, and remembering the survivability filter from Chapter 5: your first property must be one whose total failure does not end your program. Doors compound. So do mistakes with mortgages on them.

T: The full playbook, in the order it pays: depreciation claimed properly from year one, on records that support it. The exit modeled at entry, gain plus recapture, so the sale price of the strategy is known in advance. The 1031 evaluated before every sale, intermediary in place before closing, clocks calendared in ink. Cost segregation priced on purchases large enough to justify it. The hold-to-step-up option weighed in the same conversation as the estate plan, per Chapter 13. And all of it licensed, as always, by Chapter 6's foundation: contemporaneous records, clean books per property, and a professional who hears about the sale before the closing, not after. In no other chapter of this book is the before so literally priced in dollars per day.

The Quarter Lens

Q2: The first-door quarter, and the patience test. The barbecue stories peak here, the fear of missing out peaks here, and the correct Q2 move is the unglamorous one: build the reserve, learn the spreadsheet, underwrite ten properties on paper before bidding on one, and buy the boring door that cash flows over the impressive one that photographs. A first property bought right in Q2 has decades of tenants paying principal ahead of it. Bought wrong, it eats the exact gap that every other chapter needs.

Q3: The stacking quarter. Equity from early doors becomes down payments on later ones, the 1031 becomes the tool that trades up without tax friction, cost segregation starts penciling at Q3 purchase prices, and the portfolio either becomes a system, with management, reserves, and books, or becomes a second job that owns the owner. Q3 is also when concentration deserves an honest look: all doors, one city, one asset class is a story with a single plot twist.

Q4: The harvest decisions: sell and pay, exchange and continue, or hold for the step-up, each with a different tax bill and a different heir experience, decided best years early, in the same room as the estate plan. Q4 landlording also gets honest about hours: the property that was passive at forty is a part-time job at seventy, and management fees stop being an expense and start being a retirement plan.

Overtime: Property is the classic transferring asset, and the classic family detonator when Chapter 13 was skipped: the unclear title, the sibling-shared house nobody can agree to sell, the basis records nobody kept. A property that transfers with a step-up, clear title, and a findable file is a legacy. The same property without them is a lawsuit with a lawn.

The Move to Make Now

Not yet an owner: build the machine before the search. This month, construct the real spreadsheet as a reusable template, every line above, and underwrite five actual listings through it, no intent to buy, pure repetitions, because the discipline is a muscle and open houses are not the gym. Set the survivability number, the maximum first-property exposure your program can absorb, in writing, before any agent gets your phone number.

Already an owner: three audits this quarter. The truth audit: run every door through the real spreadsheet at current taxes, insurance, and honest maintenance, and meet your actual portfolio. The reserve audit: a funded account per property, sized to the systems' ages, no exceptions. The records audit: depreciation claimed correctly from day one, basis and improvements documented, books separated, and if any answer is no, that is the assignment before the next acquisition, not after.

Thinking of selling anything, ever: this is the one move with a literal price per day. Before listing, before accepting any offer, run the exit math, gain plus recapture, and the 1031 analysis with your professional, intermediary identified in advance. Sixty days early is a strategy. One day late is a donation.

The Warning

Real estate has the most sophisticated fantasy industry of any asset class in this book, and it is aimed directly at your Q2. The courses selling no-money-down empires, the gurus with rented Lamborghinis and leased confidence, the seminar math where every tenant pays, every month, forever, and every market only rises. Run all of it through the boring questions from Chapter 5: show me the actual cash flow, the actual vacancy, the actual downside, and watch the fantasy require urgency to survive the questions. Real properties survive boring questions. That is how you know they are real.

And the second warning belongs to the spreadsheet itself: it only protects the person who refuses to negotiate with it. The most common casualty in this chapter is not the fool who never ran numbers. It is the buyer who ran them, watched the property fail the math, and then adjusted the assumptions until it passed, the rent nudged up, the vacancy deleted, the maintenance halved, because they had already fallen in love and the spreadsheet was the last thing standing at the altar. The Genius from Chapter 20 does this in ink and calls it underwriting. The number said no. Hear this as an operator: the spreadsheet is not the obstacle to the deal. The spreadsheet is the only friend in the room, and no one is bigger than the program, including the program's author standing in a very charming duplex.

The Checklist

☐ Build the real spreadsheet template: rent, vacancy, PITI, maintenance, capital reserve, management

☐ Underwrite five live listings as repetitions before any offer

☐ Set the first-property survivability number in writing

☐ Fund a dedicated reserve account per property, sized to system ages

☐ Confirm depreciation is claimed properly from year one, on supportable records

The Before 40 Club Rule

Buy the spreadsheet, not the story. The code rewards landlords who read the rules before the closing, and invoices everyone else.

One question before you go. Am I underwriting the spreadsheet or the story?

Put this chapter to work in the companion Before 40 Club Workbook at before40club.com.

CHAPTER 15:

BEFORE YOU TAKE OR GIVE EQUITY

The Expensive Lesson

Somewhere out there is a founder who will sell a company in seven years for more money than their family has ever seen, and the size of the check they actually keep was decided this morning, in a formation document they clicked through, in an election window they have never heard of, on a clock that started without a sound.

Equity is the asset class where the before in Before 40 Club is measured in years and priced in millions. Every other chapter's mistakes bill you in thousands and correct in seasons. Equity mistakes bill at exit scale and mostly cannot be corrected at all, because the tax code's biggest gifts to builders, and they are enormous, genuinely, the largest legal tax breaks a working person can touch, are all structured the same way: decided early, held long, and forfeited silently by people who did not know they were holding anything.

The expensive lesson comes in one sentence: with equity, the paperwork is the strategy. Not the hustle, not the valuation, not the pitch deck. The entity chosen at formation, the one-page election filed inside a window measured in days, the five-year clock nobody announces, the cap table kept clean or tangled. Founders lose more at exit to bad early structure than to any bad deal, and the cruelest part is the timing of the discovery: the mistakes are made in week one, invisible for years, and revealed at the exact moment they can no longer be fixed, by an acquirer's diligence team reading your company's history back to you with a calculator.

This chapter covers all three seats at the equity table: the founder giving it, the employee taking it, and the angel buying it. Different seats, same rulebook, same discipline: read it before, because after does not exist here.

The Story

Keeping everything legally sensitive off this page, here is the shape of what I see from both chairs. If you decide to build a venture-backed company, the paperwork is the strategy from the first day: the right trusted advisors, a term sheet you actually understand, liquidation preferences you have read twice, because those clauses decide who gets paid at the exit and founders sign them at the moment of maximum excitement and minimum attention.

And from the CPA chair, the employee version of this chapter walks in constantly. One of my clients works at a major AI company headed toward a public offering, and the work we did together is exactly the unglamorous machinery this chapter preaches: updating the W-4 before the equity events instead of after, choosing the right elections on the right timeline, mapping the tax consequence of every vesting and every potential exercise before the liquidity exists, so the bill never arrives ahead of the money. The vocabulary that decides these outcomes is small and unforgiving: the Section 83(b) election and its window, Section 1202 and the QSBS exclusion, Section 1045 rollovers for keeping qualified gains qualified. None of it is exotic. All of it is calendared. In equity, I will say it again because it is the rule of the chapter: the paperwork is the strategy, and the clocks only start for people who start them.

The through-line in every equity scar I have ever reviewed: the information was knowable at the moment of decision, the professional was affordable relative to the stakes, and the founder was too busy building to read the rules of the thing they were building. Speed is a virtue everywhere in a startup except the paperwork. In the paperwork, speed is how you donate the exit.

What Nobody Told You

Nobody told you that the entity decision at formation is the exit decision

Chapter 10 drew the fork and this chapter prices it: if the path is venture, investment, scale, exit, the C corporation from day one is not a preference, it is the doorway to everything below, because institutional investors expect it, equity plumbing assumes it, and the largest prize in this chapter, the qualified small business stock exclusion, requires it. Founders who start as LLCs to keep it simple and convert later may start certain clocks later than they had to, and clocks, you are about to learn, are the entire game here. The lifestyle path from Chapter 10 remains completely legitimate. But choose it or leave it on purpose, because the default choice, whatever a website's dropdown suggested, is still a choice, and it compounds.

Nobody told you about QSBS, the largest legal tax break most founders never claim

Plain English: qualified small business stock is a provision that can make millions of dollars of gain on the sale of qualifying startup stock federally tax-free. Not deferred. Excluded. The headline requirements: original shares in a C corporation that was small enough when the shares were issued, running an active qualifying business, and, the big one, held for five years before the sale. The exclusion is capped, but the cap is enormous, per taxpayer, per company, and planning at real estates can extend it further. Now the parts that fill my office with quiet grief: the five-year clock starts when you acquire the shares, which is why formation date and early paperwork decide exits half a decade later. The silent disqualifiers are real, certain corporate actions, certain redemptions, drifting past the asset threshold, the wrong kind of business activity, and they trigger without ceremony, discovered only in diligence. And the states do not all play along: some conform to the federal exclusion and some tax the gain anyway, which changes the math of where and how. QSBS is not just for founders, early employees exercising options and angels buying original shares can qualify too, which is why every seat at this table should know the acronym cold. If any equity in your life could ever be worth real money, the QSBS status question belongs in writing, from a professional, this year. It is the single highest-leverage question in this book.

Nobody told you the 83(b) election exists, and its window does not forgive

Founders and early employees often receive stock that vests over time, and the tax code offers a one-page choice: file the 83(b) election, generally within thirty days of the grant, and you elect to be taxed on the stock's value now, while it is worth almost nothing, converting all future growth into capital gain territory and starting your holding clocks immediately. Skip it, and as the shares vest while the company grows, each vesting can be taxable income at the new, higher value, a recurring tax event on paper wealth you cannot sell, compounding exactly as the company succeeds. The form is one page. The window is roughly thirty days from the grant, and it is one of the few deadlines in the entire code with essentially no mercy for the late. The filing costs an envelope. The missed filing has cost people fortunes. If restricted stock is anywhere in your life, this paragraph is an emergency until the question is answered in writing.

Nobody told you what you actually signed, employee edition

The offer letter said equity and you heard rich, and between those two words sits a vocabulary that decides your outcome. Options are the right to buy shares at a set price, worth something only above that price, and exercising them can itself be a tax event, with the two flavors, incentive and non-qualified, taxed on different schedules, one of them capable of triggering tax on paper gains you have not sold, the classic scar of the last several booms. Restricted stock units are simpler and blunter: shares that become income at vesting, taxed then, at your rates, whether or not you sell, Chapter 12's concentration warning included at no charge. The employee playbook in four lines: know which instrument you hold, know what exercising or vesting costs in tax before the event, never exercise a life-changing amount without professional math on the same table, and treat vested employer stock as Chapter 12 taught, a position that must justify staying, not one that needs permission to leave.

Nobody told you what a SAFE is and is not, or what dilution actually does

For founders raising and angels writing checks: a SAFE or convertible note is not stock yet. It is an agreement that becomes stock later, at the next priced round, under terms, caps and discounts, that decide how much. That matters twice: the holding clocks that power the tax treatments above generally start when you own actual shares, not paper that will become shares, and the founder stacking SAFEs without modeling the conversion is scheduling a surprise for the exact morning the priced round closes, when all of them convert at once and the ownership math lands. Dilution itself is not a villain, it is the price of fuel, but it is a price founders must model per round, because twenty percent of something is the plan and the founders who end with three percent of their own company mostly got there without ever once running the spreadsheet. Clean cap table, modeled rounds, actual share dates known. That is the whole hygiene.

And nobody told the angels that the tax code softens startup losses, if you know the rules going in

The honest base rate first: most angel checks go to zero, and anyone who tells you otherwise is selling something. The code knows this, and it built tools for people who read it. Section 1244, in plain English, can let losses on qualifying small business stock be deducted against ordinary income rather than trapped in the capital loss rules, a meaningfully better outcome in the likely case. QSBS, from above, can make the rare winner federally tax-free, the best outcome in the unlikely case. Between those two provisions, the tax code is effectively subsidizing both tails of angel investing for the investor who structures correctly and keeps records, and doing nothing for the one who wires money on vibes. Add the discipline the math demands, many small checks rather than three large ones, because the winners must pay for the field, and basis and paperwork tracked from day one, because an exit with no records is a tax mess with a celebration attached, and you have the entire responsible angel playbook. Structure beats luck. Luck is not listening anyway.

The C.A.T. Breakdown

C: Equity is the asset class most hostile to cash flow, and pretending otherwise is the scar factory. It is illiquid for years, its tax events, exercises, vestings, conversions, arrive on their own schedule and demand real cash against paper wealth, and Chapter 4's reserve discipline is the only thing standing between an employee and the exercise-tax ambush. The rules: never spend paper gains, never plan a lifestyle on unvested anything, fund every equity tax event from the reserve with the math done first, and for angels, invest only what the gap can lose in full without the program noticing, because the base rate says it will.

A: Equity is Chapter 5 at maximum voltage: the purest form of owning something that earns without your hours, and the most concentrated single point of failure a portfolio can hold. Both are true at once, and the discipline is holding both: build and take equity aggressively, because it is how outsized outcomes happen, and diversify it on written rules as it becomes real, because Chapter 12 already met the person whose paycheck and portfolio shared one logo. For founders, the A-work is Chapter 10's conversion at company scale, systems, records, clean structure, because an acquirer buys the transferable asset, and diligence prices every shortcut you took at ten times what the shortcut saved.

T: This chapter is the T chapter of the entire book, so here is the consolidated calendar. At formation or grant: entity chosen for the declared path, 83(b) analyzed within its thirty-day window, QSBS status confirmed in writing, share dates documented. During the build: clocks tracked, silent disqualifiers reviewed before any redemption or corporate action, cap table kept clean, basis records kept current, exercises and vestings tax-modeled before they happen, not after. Before the exit: the QSBS file assembled, the state conformity question answered, the timing of the sale held against the five-year clock, because closing four months early has cost people seven figures for the privilege of impatience. Every item is boring. Every item is worth more than any negotiation you will ever conduct. The paperwork is the strategy.

The Quarter Lens

Q2: The formation quarter, where nearly every clock in this chapter starts, and the quarter with the worst information environment: founders too broke for advice at exactly the moment advice is worth the most. Hear the arithmetic: the professional review at formation costs a few thousand dollars against a possible seven-figure swing at exit, the single best-priced insurance in this book. Q2 employees taking startup offers owe themselves the vocabulary above before signing, because the offer letter is a tax document wearing a congratulations.

Q3: The harvest and concentration quarter. Exits land here, on structures set in Q2, and the difference between the founder who filed the page and the founder who did not is now a number with commas. Q3 is also when equity wealth must become portfolio wealth, the diversification rules executed, the single logo retired, because a Q3 net worth concentrated in one company is a Q2 risk profile without the Q2 runway.

Q4: Equity turns into legacy machinery: the step-up from Chapter 13 meets appreciated shares, charitable strategies meet low-basis stock, and the question becomes transfer design. Angels in Q4 shift from writing checks to structuring what the checks became.

Overtime: Founders' shares, tracked and titled properly, transfer as clean assets. The alternative, certificates in a drawer, basis nobody recorded, entities nobody dissolved, is Chapter 13's kitchen-table problem with a cap table attached. The company outlives the founder only on paper that was kept.

The Move to Make Now

If you hold or are about to receive any equity, this week, one page per position: what instrument, exactly, acquired or granted on what date, what clocks are running, 83(b) filed or analyzed or missed, QSBS status confirmed or unknown, what the next tax event is and what it will cost in cash. Any box marked unknown is the assignment, and the 83(b) box, if a grant is inside thirty days, is the assignment today, before dinner.

If you are forming a company this year: declare the path per Chapter 10, and if it is venture, the sequence is C corporation at formation, 83(b) analysis on every founder's stock inside the window, QSBS eligibility confirmed in writing, cap table software from day one, and a professional who has done startup work reviewing all of it before the first outside dollar. Total cost, a rounding error on the round. Total value, potentially the majority of your exit.

If you are angel investing or about to: write the policy before the next check. The annual amount the gap can lose entirely, the check size that forces diversification across many bets, the structural questions asked before wiring, actual shares or converting paper, 1244 and QSBS status, and the records file opened per investment. Angels with a written policy are investors. Angels without one are Chapter 20 donors with better vocabulary.

The Warning

The equity world runs on a mythology of speed, move fast, close fast, paperwork later, and the mythology is half right: product, hiring, and sales reward speed. The paperwork does not. The paperwork rewards the founder who slowed down for one week in week one, and it fines everyone else at exit, with interest measured in years of clocks that started late or never. When the culture around you says handle the legal stuff later, hear it as Chapter 6 taught you to hear everything: later is April, and April is too late, except here April is five years long and arrives exactly once.

And the seat-specific warnings, one each. Founders: the Goofball's co-founder scar from Chapter 20 lives in this chapter's jurisdiction, equity splits decided on friendship, vesting skipped between people who trusted each other, and the misaligned person from that chapter is never more expensive than when they hold your stock, so paper the partnership while you like each other, which is the only time you can. Employees: the company that pays you is not your financial advisor, and the exercise decision that changes your life deserves math from someone whose paycheck does not depend on your morale. Angels: the deal that cannot wait for your structural questions has answered them. Nobody cares more than you will, and in this chapter, caring is spelled p-a-p-e-r-w-o-r-k.

The Checklist

☐ One page per equity position: instrument, dates, clocks, elections, QSBS status, next tax event
☐ Any grant inside thirty days: 83(b) analysis completed today, filed if indicated
☐ QSBS status on every plausible position confirmed in writing by a professional
☐ Venture-path formations: C corporation, founder stock papered, vesting on everyone, cap table software from day one
☐ Model every exercise and vesting for tax before the event, funded from the reserve

The Before 40 Club Rule

In equity, the paperwork is the strategy. The exit is decided at the entrance, and the clocks only start for people who start them.

One question before you go. Which clock in my equity life has already started without me?

Put this chapter to work in the companion Before 40 Club Workbook at before40club.com.

PART III:
THE PLAYER

Five chapters about the person holding the book. The offense, the rooms, the posture, the builder, and the goofball in the mirror. The method from Part I and the exams from Part II are run by a player, and this part upgrades the player.

CHAPTER 16:

MMM: MAKE MORE MONEY

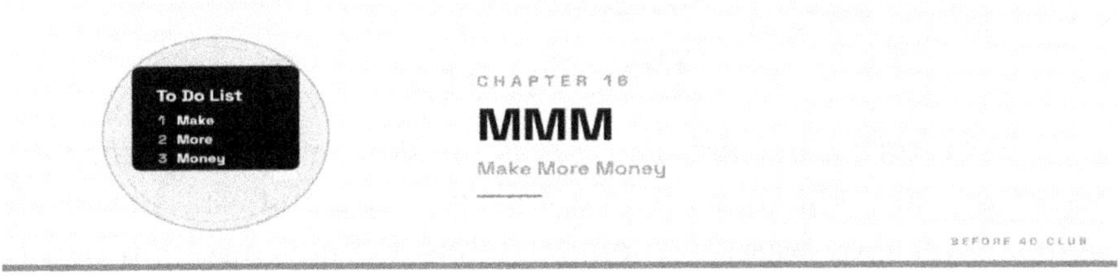

"The first $1,000 comes from work. The first $100,000 comes from skill. The first $1 million comes from systems."

The Expensive Lesson

Somewhere in the last fifteen chapters, a certain kind of reader started to squirm, and this chapter exists because they are right to.

The squirm sounds like this: I have run the truth layer, I have cut the leaks, my gap is honest, and my honest gap is small. The reserve math works, but it works slowly. The asset math works, but at my numbers it is a thirty-year sentence. Everything in this book is correct, and at my income, correct is not enough.

Good. That squirm is the most productive discomfort in personal finance, because it has located the wall that the entire budgeting industry pretends does not exist: cutting has a floor. You can only reduce your expenses to zero, and you will quit the program long before you get anywhere near it, because a life optimized purely for smallness is a life people abandon, and they should. But earning has no ceiling. There is no law of mathematics, markets, or nature that caps what you can make, and every chapter in this book gets more powerful with more fuel: a bigger gap buys assets faster, a bigger reserve buys calm cheaper, and every tax strategy in Chapter 6 is worth more at higher numbers.

So here is the flag of this chapter, three letters that belong next to C.A.T. in your permanent vocabulary: MMM. Make More Money. Not as a hustle-culture slogan, and not as a substitute for the system, Chapter 12 already showed you what more money does to a broken bucket. MMM is the second blade of the scissors. Defense makes money stay. Offense makes money arrive. The people who get free run both blades, and the expensive lesson is that most people spend their whole lives sharpening only one, clipping coupons with a scissor that cannot cut.

The Story

Two stories, one arc. The first is the skill bet. I did my master's in taxation at Fordham part-time while working, and what the degree actually installed was the connective tissue: entity taxation tied to personal livelihood, the realization that every single life event carries a tax consequence, single, married, divorced, buying a home, selling one, and that a person who never learns this is playing every round of their life with a handicap. Meanwhile the day jobs were the laboratory. At KKR I watched deals and structures move and saw that there is always a tax component, always. At Five Oaks I studied what leadership costs and what it changes. I was being paid a salary to acquire the exact judgment I would later sell at multiples of it, which is the entire MMM thesis in one sentence.

The second story is the repricing, and it started with a realization: an accounting firm is secretly a SaaS business. Build a book of one hundred business clients paying two thousand dollars a month and you are running recurring software revenue with a human interface. That reframe killed the hourly model at my firm, because hours are the one input I cannot manufacture more of, your time is the finite item, and moved everything to value-based pricing. Offense is not hustle. Offense is understanding what your judgment is worth, packaging it so it scales, and refusing to sell the only asset with a hard ceiling, which is your hours.

The pattern under every MMM story I have lived or witnessed: the income was available before the courage was. The market was ready to pay more before the earner was ready to ask. Which means the bottleneck in most incomes is not the economy, the industry, or the boss. It is a conversation the earner keeps not having, and this chapter is going to schedule it.

What Nobody Told You

Nobody told you that income is a price, and prices are set by whoever speaks first

Your salary is not a measurement of your worth. It is the number that survived a negotiation you probably did not know you were in, set against a budget you never saw, by someone whose job was to pay the least you would accept. Every year you do not renegotiate, you are accepting last year's price for this year's more experienced product, and inflation is quietly running a discount on top. The employed reader's first MMM move is the least glamorous one: the documented case, your results in numbers, the market rate researched for real, and the conversation requested on purpose, not waited for. Most raises are not refused. They are unrequested. And if the honest market research says your employer's ceiling is below your market price, the research just wrote your next move for you.

Nobody told you to raise your prices before you feel ready, because ready is not a price signal

For the self-employed, the freelancers, the firm owners: your prices are almost certainly set by your comfort, not your market, and your comfort was calibrated years ago by the broke version of you who was grateful for anything. Here is the test that costs nothing: if every client says yes instantly, your price is wrong. Instant unanimous yes means you are the discount, and the discount works twice as hard for half the position. Raising prices is the highest-margin move in business, every additional dollar is pure profit on work you were already doing, and the fear surrounding it is almost always a Chapter 2 default wearing a business case. Raise them on the next new client, then on the next renewal, and let the market, not your childhood, tell you where the ceiling is. Fire a bad client at least once, and learn what it teaches you: that the capacity they consumed was an asset you were donating.

Nobody told you that skills are the assets nobody can repossess

Chapter 5 gave you the asset families, and this chapter adds the one that lives in your head: a priced skill, meaning a skill the market visibly pays for, is an income-generating asset with no property tax, no tenants, and no market crash. The MMM discipline is to invest in skills the way Chapter 5 invests in assets: deliberately, near your existing edge, with the survivability filter on. The highest-paying skill stack in almost every field is the same two-layer combination: your technical craft, plus the ability to sell it, communicate it, or lead with it. Learn to sell, or partner with someone who can, because the unsold skill is inventory, not income, and the market pays for what it can see.

Nobody told you the difference between a second job and a second engine

When the gap needs to grow, most people reach for the obvious: more hours, a second shift, a gig app, which is renting out more of the exact inventory Chapter 5 told you was the worst on earth. Sometimes that is the right short-term move, cash is cash, and a season of extra hours pointed at a specific target, the reserve, the down payment, the debt, is honest work with an end date. But hear the distinction: a second job rents more hours. A second engine builds toward income that eventually detaches from hours: the practice on the side, the product, the content, the small service business, the thing that starts as hours and is designed, on purpose, to become an asset. Same evening, two different futures. If you are going to spend your surplus hours, spend them on something with a conversion plan, because Chapter 10 is standing by to structure it the moment it earns its first real dollar.

And nobody told you the rule that keeps MMM from becoming the trap: new money enters the old pipes

Chapter 12 met the high earners whose raises evaporated into lifestyle, and their disease started as healthy MMM with no plumbing. The rule, mechanical and non-negotiable: every MMM win, the raise, the new client, the side income, flows through the Chapter 4 system before you ever feel it, the capture rule taking its half, the reserve taking its percentage, the conversion machine taking its cut, and only the remainder reaching the lifestyle. MMM without the system is louder brokeness on a delay. MMM through the system is the fastest wealth-building force available to a working person, because it attacks the only side of the equation with no ceiling.

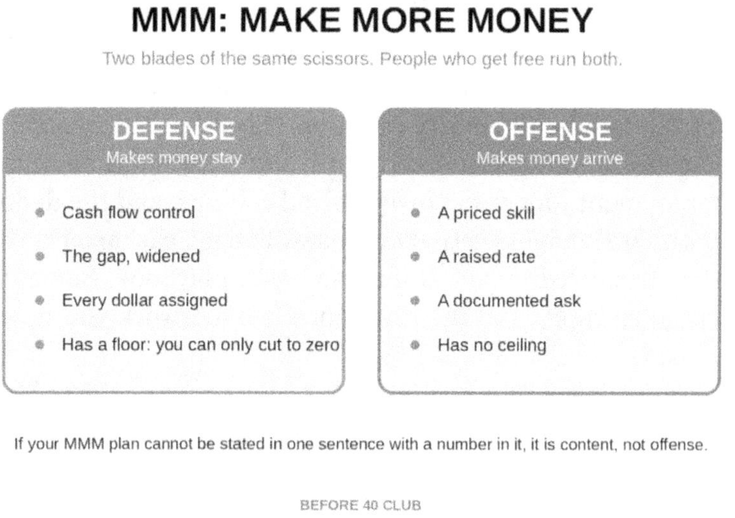

MMM: defense makes money stay, offense makes money arrive

The C.A.T. Breakdown

C: MMM is the offense of cash flow, and it obeys cash flow discipline: every new income stream gets its own truth layer, real revenue, real costs, real hours, because a side income that nets four dollars an hour after honest accounting is a hobby taxing your sleep. And the capture rule governs everything: the raise, the new contract, the windfall, half to the gap before it lands, automated, forever. The earner who captures their increases becomes wealthy on the same career their neighbor spends.

A: Every MMM stream should be interrogated with the Chapter 5 question on a schedule: is this still renting hours, or is it converting? The freelance practice becomes an agency with systems. The expertise becomes the course, the book, the product. The side hustle becomes the Chapter 10 business with real structure. Not every stream must convert, some hours-for-money at a great rate is a fine engine, but every stream should be asked, annually, and the ones with conversion potential should get the investment. Your income statement is supposed to migrate, over the quarters, from hours to assets, and MMM is the migration's fuel.

T: New income is a tax event before it is a lifestyle event, and the MMM reader must hear Chapter 4 and Chapter 10 in stereo: side income arrives with no withholding, which means the reserve percentage and the estimated rhythm start with the first invoice, not the first scary letter. And new income at new levels reopens every Chapter 6 analysis: the entity question once the side income is real, the S election math at the new profit, the retirement accounts that self-employment unlocks at owner-sized ceilings, and the deductions that legitimate business activity licenses. The raise is taxed at your top rate; the structured business income has a playbook. Same dollars, different keep rates, and the difference is paperwork you now know how to read.

The Quarter Lens

Q2: The MMM quarter of life. Energy is at maximum, obligations at minimum, and every additional dollar earned has the longest compounding runway it will ever have. Q2 is when the skill stack gets built, the pricing courage gets trained, and the second engine gets started in the evenings, and it is also when the comparison trap burns hottest, so aim the ambition at the gap, not the feed. A Q2 that adds one priced skill and one converting income stream changes every quarter after it.

Q3: The leverage quarter. Your Q2 reputation, network, and skills are now assets that can be priced at their peak, and Q3 MMM looks less like more hours and more like better terms: the senior rate, the equity component, the business that scales, the pricing power of a proven name. Q3 is also the last cheap decade to convert hours into assets, which makes coasting the most expensive comfortable decision available.

Q4: MMM matures into selectivity: the consulting at chosen rates, the board seat, the licensing of a lifetime's expertise, income streams that respect the calendar of a person who no longer sells hours. The Q4 earners with options are, universally, the ones whose earlier MMM was converted, not just collected.

Overtime: Skills die with the owner, but converted skills, the business, the book, the brand, the systems, keep earning. The final MMM question is the Chapter 5 question at the end of the road: how much of what you knew became something that outlasts you?

The Move to Make Now

Three moves, thirty days, pick the version that matches your seat.

Employed: build the case file this month, your documented results in numbers, the real market rate from actual postings and actual peers, and the specific ask. Schedule the conversation, on purpose, within thirty days. Whatever the answer, you exit with information: the raise, or the market research that becomes your move.

Self-employed: raise your price on the next new client, this month, by more than feels comfortable, and watch what actually happens instead of what fear predicted. Simultaneously, run the truth layer on your client list and identify the one whose fully-loaded cost, hours, stress, scope creep, makes them your lowest-margin account, and begin the exit. Capacity is an asset. Reclaim it, then re-price it.

Everyone: pick the one skill that, added to your current stack, most raises your market price, apply the proximity and survivability filters from Chapter 5, and put real hours against it weekly, with a ninety-day checkpoint. And write the second-engine thesis in one paragraph, what it is, what it costs to start, its conversion plan, even if the start date is next quarter. A written engine gets built. A vague one gets discussed at barbecues for a decade.

And all of it through the pipes: before any new income arrives, confirm the capture rule, the reserve percentage, and the conversion transfer are automated and waiting. Build the plumbing before the rain.

The Warning

MMM has a counterfeit, and it is everywhere: the hustle performance, the 4am posts, the seven streams of income listicle, the grind cosplay that confuses exhaustion with progress. Real MMM is boring and specific: a priced skill, a raised rate, a documented ask, an engine with a conversion plan. If your MMM plan cannot be stated in one sentence with a number in it, it is content, not offense. The Office Rat, whom you will meet fully in Chapter 18, has a hustle mode too, and it produces the same thing his office mode produces: visible effort, invisible results.

And the second warning, the one this book will not let you skip: MMM is the second blade, never the first. The reader who felt the squirm and skips back to offense without finishing defense is pouring faster into the leaking bucket, and Chapter 12 is full of people who won the income game and lost the keeping game. Run the order the book runs it: truth layer, pipes, reserve, then offense at full aggression. Income exposes your system. Build the system, then go get the income that deserves it. Nobody caps your earning but the market, and the market has never once been the thing that was actually in the way.

The Checklist

☐ Employed: case file built, market rate researched, conversation scheduled within 30 days

☐ Self-employed: price raised on the next new client, this month

☐ Identify and begin exiting the lowest-margin client or commitment

☐ Choose the one skill that most raises your market price; schedule weekly hours against it

☐ Write the second-engine thesis: one paragraph, one number, one conversion plan

The Before 40 Club Rule

Cutting has a floor. Earning has no ceiling. Sharpen both blades, and run every new dollar through the pipes.

One question before you go. What would I charge if I priced my judgment instead of my hours?

Agency: Your rate, your skill hours, and your ask are all yours. Which one moves first? **Urgency:** What is the date of the conversation, the price change, or the first offer, this month?

Put this chapter to work in the companion Before 40 Club Workbook at before40club.com.

CHAPTER 17:

GAS: GET AROUND STRANGERS

"Put yourself in the room."

The Expensive Lesson

Here is an audit nobody runs, and it prices higher than any account you hold: list the last five significant opportunities of your life, the job, the client, the deal, the introduction, the idea that changed your trajectory, and next to each one, write down where it came from.

I have asked versions of that question across a desk for years, and the answers converge on a pattern that should rearrange your calendar: almost none of it came from your closest circle, and almost none of it came from strangers on the internet either. It came from the middle ring, the people you sort of knew, the former colleague, the friend of a friend, the person from the room you almost did not attend. Sociologists have a name for this, the strength of weak ties, and the plain-English version is the thesis of this chapter: opportunities travel through rooms, and they travel fastest through rooms you are new in.

Why? Because your inner circle, the people you love most, mostly knows what you know, sees what you see, and hears about the jobs, deals, and ideas you already heard about. Their information overlaps yours almost completely; that overlap is what makes them close. Strangers and near-strangers carry non-overlapping information: the industry you have not considered, the client who needs exactly you, the financing structure you did not know existed, the standard of what is normal that quietly raises yours. Chapter 2 taught you that your defaults were installed by your environment.

This chapter is the adult sequel: your environment is still installing you, every week, and unlike Q1, you now pick the environment.

So add the third acronym to the permanent vocabulary: GAS. Get Around Strangers. Deliberately, regularly, strategically, and with standards. The expensive lesson is that most people's networks stop growing the year they get comfortable, and from that year forward, their opportunities, information, and normals are all running on inventory, aging in place, while they wonder why the breaks seem to go to people who get out more. The breaks do not go to people who get out more. They go through them, because rooms are how the breaks move.

The Story

The room that changed me was Queen City Fintech. Over a hundred companies applied, six got in, and I flew to Charlotte and lived there for roughly three months, a New York CPA dropped into a city where I knew nobody, surrounded by founders and bankers who owed me nothing. That is the whole formula of this chapter, executed literally: I put myself in a room full of strangers and let the room work.

And the room worked. I met one of the early leaders at Credit Karma Tax, the product that became Cash App Taxes, exactly the kind of person a tax-software founder needs in his orbit and exactly the kind of person who does not exist inside your existing circle. Beyond any single introduction, those three months expanded my sense of what the path could even look like, which is the quietest and most valuable thing rooms do. And here is the honest accounting, because GAS deserves honest books: some of the opportunities from that season did not pan out. That is fine. That is the design. Rooms are reps, and reps compound, and you can never predict which conversation is the one carrying the next five years in its pocket. You just have to keep being in rooms where that conversation is possible.

The uncomfortable arithmetic in every version of that story: the opportunity existed before I entered the room. It was already circulating, already funded, already looking for someone, and my absence from the room was the only thing between us. Talent that nobody with resources knows about is, economically speaking, indistinguishable from no talent. That sentence is unfair and true, and GAS is the response to it.

What Nobody Told You

Nobody told you that your network is an asset class, and it obeys asset rules

Run it through Chapter 5's definition: does it earn without your hours? A real network does, continuously, referrals arriving while you sleep, your name spoken in rooms you are not in, information reaching you before it reaches the market. And like every asset, it compounds, requires deliberate contributions, decays when ignored, and cannot be bought in bulk the week you need it. The person who starts networking during the job search is the person who starts saving during the emergency, and both discover the same thing: this asset only accepts deposits in advance.

Nobody told you that GAS has a currency, and the currency is value given first

Here is why most people hate networking and why what they hate is not this chapter: they picture extraction, the card-thrusting, favor-hunting, what-can-you-do-for-me performance, and they are right to hate it, because extraction does not compound, it burns. The actual mechanics of a working network run the opposite direction: you become the person who gives first, the introduction made with nothing asked, the useful thing sent because it was useful, the expertise shared freely at the edges, and in your case, in mine, the CPA who answers the small question generously, and deposits accumulate in an account you cannot see until it starts paying, and then it never stops. Give first, track nothing, and let the compounding be invisible until it is not. That is not idealism. Eighteen years in, it is the highest-ROI behavior I have ever practiced.

Nobody told you that rooms have tiers, and you should be slightly out of your depth in at least one

There are rooms where you are the most accomplished person present, and they are comfortable, affirming, and developmentally worthless. There are rooms where you are roughly average, and they are where community lives. And there are rooms where you are, honestly, the least impressive person there, and those rooms are where your normals get recalibrated: what people at the next level consider a reasonable price, a reasonable goal, a reasonable year. You need all three, but ambition lives in the third, and the third is precisely the room your comfort will vote against attending, every time, with excellent excuses. Book it anyway. Discomfort in the right room is tuition; comfort in the wrong one is also tuition, just invisible and compounding.

Nobody told you the introvert clause, so let me write it in

GAS is not a personality requirement, and this chapter is not asking you to become the loudest person at a mixer. It is asking for exposure to non-overlapping people, and exposure has quiet formats: the small dinner instead of the conference floor, the one-on-one coffee instead of the panel crowd, the online community where your written expertise travels, the niche event where your specific craft is the conversation. The introvert who has three real conversations at a small gathering beats the extrovert who collected forty cards, because networks are built on remembered exchanges, not contact volume. Get around strangers in whatever format your wiring sustains. The only disqualified format is none.

And nobody told you that GAS without standards is just the Goofball outsourcing his circle

Chapter 20 warned you that a misaligned person is an expensive liability, and new rooms are full of candidates: the operators who work rooms for prey, the association-collectors, the impressive-sounding people whose deals never quite close. GAS and curation are one discipline, not two: expand the surface area, then filter hard on alignment, the values, the standards, the way they talk about the people who are not present. The filter question that has served me: does this person make me sharper, calmer, or better resourced, or do they make me spend, doubt, or perform? Expand aggressively. Admit selectively. The goal was never a bigger circle. The goal is a better-supplied one.

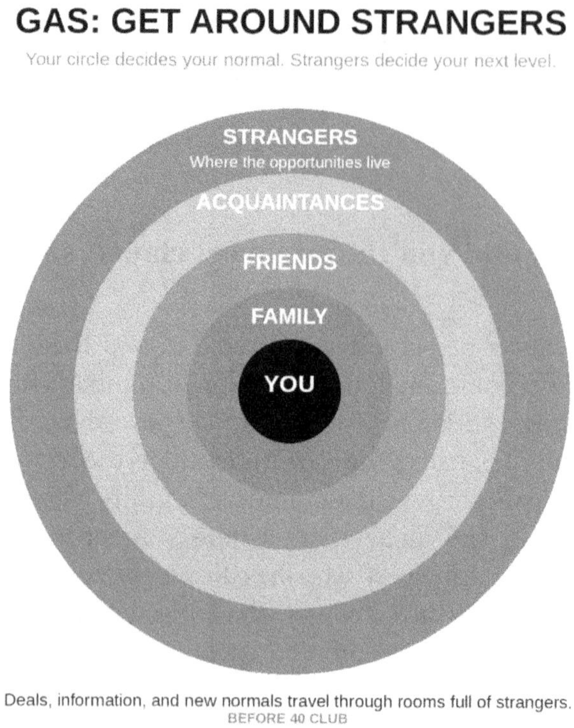

GAS: your circle decides your normal, strangers decide your next level

The C.A.T. Breakdown

C: GAS is a budget line, and treating it as one is what separates the deliberate from the occasional: the memberships, the events, the travel to the right rooms, the dinners you host, funded from the gap, on purpose, as an investment with an honest annual number attached. And run the truth layer on it like any investment: which rooms, over a year, actually produced relationships, information, or opportunities, and which were networking theater with a ticket price? Double the former. Cancel the latter. Relationship capital deserves the same auditing as every other deployment of the gap.

A: The network is the asset that appreciates every other asset. Deals from Chapter 14 travel through rooms before they hit the market. Capital from Chapter 15 moves on warm introductions almost exclusively. The Chapter 10 business grows on referrals, the Chapter

16 pricing power rests on reputation, and the career itself, the original asset, is repriced by who knows your work. Which reframes the A question of this chapter: you are not networking. You are building the distribution system for everything else you build. And like Chapter 5 said about first assets, the network you start building this year looks embarrassingly small, and the one you have in ten years is a different life.

T: Two honest notes, in this book's plain style. First, the boring one: when relationship-building is genuinely business, the industry event, the client development, the professional membership, it lives in the Chapter 10 books like every legitimate business activity, documented, real, never inflated, and the standard is the same as everywhere in Chapter 6: real purpose, real records, no costumes. Second, the larger one: some of the most valuable tax knowledge moves through rooms before it moves through publications, the planner someone recommends, the structure someone mentions, the question you did not know to ask until you heard someone at the next level ask it. I have watched a single dinner conversation reroute someone's entity structure and reprice their next decade. Rooms are where the Chapter 6 questions come from. The answers you can hire. The questions, you have to be around.

The Quarter Lens

Q2: The planting quarter for relationship capital, with the best exchange rate it will ever have: people are unusually open in Q2, hierarchies are unformed, and the peer you meet at a nothing event this year is a decision-maker in fifteen. Q2 GAS is planting a forest with saplings, and it is also the quarter comfort first calcifies, the same apartment, same crew, same weekends, so the discipline starts now: one new room per month, minimum, forever.

Q3: The harvest and the hazard. The Q2 forest pays out here, the network is now senior, resourced, and reachable, and Q3 GAS shifts from access-seeking to value-brokering: you become the introducer, the connector, the person rooms form around, which is the strongest network position there is. The hazard is the Q3 shrink: career, family, and fatigue quietly cancel the new rooms, and the network starts aging in place exactly when its compounding is steepest. Guard the one-room-per-month rule most fiercely here.

Q4: The network becomes legacy infrastructure: the doors you open for the next generation, the board rooms, the mentorship, the capital and clients you now route rather than chase. Q4 operators with maintained networks stay relevant, resourced, and independent for decades. The isolated version, however wealthy, gets stale information and worse deals, and Chapter 13 warned you who circles the isolated.

Overtime: Relationships are the one asset in this book that transfers while you are alive: the introductions made for your children, the reputation that outlives you, the rooms that remember your name because of how you behaved in them. Chapter 5 said hours die with the worker. A network, tended, does not.

The Move to Make Now

Four moves, thirty days.

One: run the opportunity audit from the top of this chapter, on paper, the last five significant breaks and their sources. Let the data tell you what your instincts have been discounting.

Two: run the circle audit, two lists. The current inner circle, each name filtered through the alignment question: sharper, calmer, better resourced, or spend, doubt, perform. And the aspiration list: five specific people or types of people one level beyond you whose rooms you are not yet in. You cannot navigate toward rooms you have not named.

Three: book the rooms, calendar, not intentions. One new room this month in the format your wiring sustains, and one room this quarter where you are honestly out of your depth, the conference, the mastermind, the dinner above your current altitude. Fund both from the gap, as investments, with the audit scheduled for year-end.

Four: make three deposits this week, value given first, nothing tracked: the introduction two people in your world should have, the useful thing sent to someone who did not ask, the generous answer to the small question in your expertise. Three deposits, every week, forever. That cadence, alone, sustained, builds the whole asset.

The Warning

Two counterfeits patrol this chapter, and both photograph well.

The first is networking theater: the events attended for the attending, the connection counts, the room-working that produces cards and content but no remembered exchanges. The test is brutal and simple: how many people from the last five events would take your call, and how many would you take? Theater optimizes the visible metrics. The asset lives entirely in the invisible one.

The second is the platform illusion: mistaking an audience for a network. Followers, connections, and subscribers are reach, and reach is genuinely valuable, I am building it myself, in public, on purpose. But reach is broadcast, and networks are exchange: reach cannot introduce you, vouch for you, or tell you the thing that is not being published. The builder needs both and confuses them at their peril, because the feed applauds while the room decides. GAS is about the rooms.

And underneath both warnings, the Chapter 20 filter stays on: new rooms mean new exposure, and your friends do not need access to your money to cost you money, a rule that applies double to impressive strangers. Expand the surface. Guard the core. Nobody cares more than you will, including about who gets close to what you are building.

The Checklist

☐ Complete the opportunity audit: last five breaks, sourced honestly

☐ Complete the circle audit: inner circle filtered, aspiration list of five named

☐ Book one new room this month, in a format your wiring sustains

☐ Book one out-of-your-depth room this quarter, funded from the gap

☐ Install the deposit cadence: three value-first gives per week, tracked nowhere

The Before 40 Club Rule

Opportunities travel through rooms. Get around strangers on purpose, give first, filter hard, and never let your circle finish growing.

One question before you go. When did I last walk into a room where nobody owed me anything?

Put this chapter to work in the companion Before 40 Club Workbook at before40club.com.

CHAPTER 18:

THE OFFICE RAT AND THE OWNER

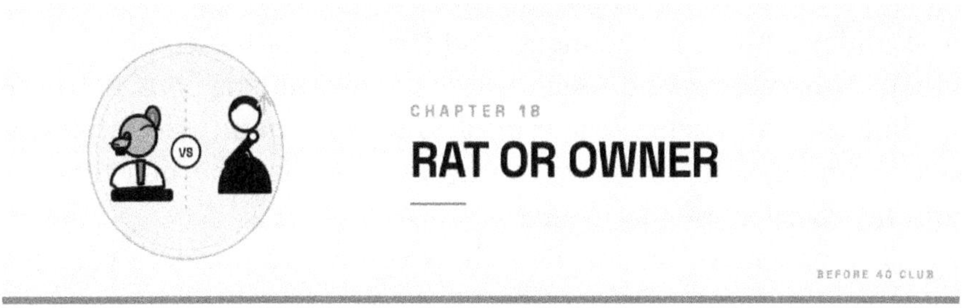

"Agency compounds. Excuses do not."

The Expensive Lesson

There are two people who can occupy the same desk, hold the same title, collect the same paycheck, and end up in two different lives, and the difference between them is invisible on the org chart.

The first one, this book has been naming all along: the Office Rat. Not an insult aimed at employees, hear that clearly, because I spent years employed at some of the most demanding institutions in finance, and some of the sharpest operators I know collect a W-2 on purpose. The Office Rat is not a job status. It is a posture: the low-agency version of a person, waiting for permission, optimizing for approval, performing effort for an audience of managers, and quietly outsourcing the ownership of their one life to an employer whose loyalty runs exactly as deep as the next budget cycle. The Office Rat can be an employee, a freelancer, or, in the saddest cases, a business owner who built a company and still waits for permission inside it.

And the Office Rat has a performance mode, so let us name that too: Ratmaxxing. The happy hour theater. The visible late nights that produce nothing but visibility. The fake urgency, the calendar full of meetings about meetings, the corporate cosplay of looking indispensable while building nothing that belongs to you, the mistake of confusing being busy with building. Ratmaxxing is optimizing for approval instead of ownership, and it has a precise cost: every hour spent performing for the org chart is an hour not spent on the gap, the skills, the second engine, or the rooms, and Chapter 5 already told you what your hours are worth and how few of them you get.

The second person at that desk is the Owner. Maybe they own a business. Maybe they own nothing yet but their posture. The Owner treats the job as a client, the paycheck as revenue, the career as an asset under active management, and their life as the company they actually run. Agency and urgency, the two words this book has been building toward: agency, the refusal to wait for permission that was never coming, and urgency, the awareness that the quarters are running whether you play or not.

The expensive lesson: nobody is coming to promote you into your own life. The employer cannot, the government will not, and the calendar does not care. The Office Rat waits. The Owner moves. Same desk. Two futures.

The Story

In 2017 I was living two lives on one calendar. The alarm went off at five in the morning and the first shift was mine: client work for the practice I was building, clients I found on Upwork and through referrals, done before the commute. Then the second shift belonged to somebody else. By day I was the controller at a mortgage REIT, and by night I was back at my own desk, building AskMyUncleSam and the firm. Sixty and seventy hour weeks, and every week ended the same way, with the Sunday blues, that low hum of dread that starts around dinner time because Monday belongs to the office. I hated it honestly. I hated the commute, I hated corporate America, and I hated what I could feel myself becoming inside it, which is exactly the animal this chapter is named after.

Here is what forced the decision, and it was not a dramatic scene. It was a quiet audit. The next position above me was CFO, the title I had been telling myself I wanted, and one day I admitted that I did not care. I did not read about REITs on my own time. I did not care about the industry. I did not care about the company beyond the paycheck. And if you study anyone great at their craft, Henry Kravis, Tom Brady, pick your example, the one thing they have in common is that they care, actually care, past the point where it is a job. I had spent two years inside the house Kravis built, so I knew what caring at that level looked like. I was never going to care like that about someone else's org chart. That is not a character flaw. That is information, and I finally read it. I was also closing in on the end of my twenties, and I understood the clock the way this book teaches it: in Q2 you do not have a lot of room for error, and every year I spent performing a role I did not want was a year of the leverage quarter spent building nothing that belonged to me.

So in October 2017 I gave notice, and I will give you the honest version of the numbers, because this chapter preaches the bridge and I want you to know why. My bridge was thinner than the one I would build you. I did not have deep savings. I had some KKR stock, a tax refund I knew was coming, ten months of the practice already running at night, and a level of misery that had become its own kind of clarity. When your back is against the wall you develop a do or die mentality, and I promised myself the day I left that I would never go back. I never have. But hear both halves of that: the fire worked for me, and I have since watched it burn plenty of people who jumped with no shift already running at five in the morning. Build the night shift first. Then jump.

What I know now, from the other side, is that there are two scripts available for every life. There is the one handed to you, and there is the one you write, and moving from the first to the second takes more quietness and more self belief than anyone tells you, because the loudest voices in your life are usually reading from the handed script. Everything that came after, the Journal, Crain's, Forbes, Muse, all of it, was already inside me during those Sunday blues years. The only thing that changed in October 2017 is that I stopped playing it safe long enough to find out.

What I carry from that season is the reframe this whole chapter runs on: the job was never the trap. The posture was. The same desk that cages the Office Rat funds the Owner's build, and the difference was never the desk.

What Nobody Told You

Nobody told you that a job is a client, and should be managed like one

The Owner's reframe, and it changes everything downstream: your employer is not your provider, your identity, or your family, whatever the onboarding deck said. Your employer is your largest client, currently buying most of your inventory at a negotiated rate. That reframe is not cynical, it is clarifying: you serve a great client excellently, you invoice at market rates, Chapter 16 showed you how, you notice when the client relationship stops serving the business, and above all, you never let one client own one hundred percent of your capacity forever, because Chapter 12 already diagnosed single-payer risk. The employee asks, how do I get promoted? The Owner asks, how is this client serving my company's strategy, and what am I building with the margin?

Nobody told you that the W-2 is venture funding for your build, if you treat it that way

Here is where this book departs from the quit-your-job carnival barking on the internet: the paycheck is the cheapest capital you will ever raise. No dilution, no investors, no interest, arriving every two weeks with benefits attached. The Owner working a job is running a funded startup: the salary covers operations, the gap from Chapter 4 becomes the investment budget, the evenings build the Chapter 16 second engine, the employer's training and rooms feed the skill stack and the network, all legitimate, all yours to keep. The Office Rat sees the paycheck as the point. The Owner sees it as the runway. Same deposit, two different balance sheets.

Nobody told you how to actually leave, so the internet did, badly

The dramatic resignation makes great content and terrible cash flow, and I have cleaned up after enough of them to write the counter-formula. Before you quit your job, four gates, in writing: the reserve at a survival horizon measured against the real truth layer, not the optimistic one, twelve months is adult, six is brave, three is content. The engine already running, real revenue from real customers, not a logo and a dream, because Chapter 10 taught you the certificate is not the business. The structure built while employed, the entity, the reserve rhythm, the books, the health insurance priced for real, because the W-2 was quietly providing infrastructure you are about to become. And the tax picture rerun for the new life, estimated payments live from the first self-employed dollar. The Owner does not leap. The Owner builds the bridge while standing on payroll, walks across, and lets the last paycheck overlap the first invoice. Agency is not recklessness. Agency with a spreadsheet is how the free actually got out.

Nobody told you that Ratmaxxing has a mirror version in the mirror

The performance trap does not end at resignation, it rebrands: the entrepreneur performing hustle instead of performing loyalty, the founder Ratmaxxing for the feed instead of the manager, busy with the aesthetics of building, the logo, the cards, the content about the grind, while the actual asset, the systems, the sales, the books, sits untouched. Chapter 16 called it hustle cosplay and this chapter names its root: the approval addiction survives the org chart, and until it is confronted, every environment becomes an office and every audience becomes a boss. The test is the same everywhere, the one from the playbook that built this book: does this activity build something I own, or does it perform something I want seen? Stop confusing being busy with building. The scoreboard from Chapter 1 does not have a column for visible effort.

And nobody told you that no one is bigger than the program, including the boss, including the brand, including you

The Office Rat secretly believes in exemptions: that loyalty will be repaid structurally, that the institution's prestige transfers to his balance sheet, that being liked is a retirement plan. The Owner knows the program is impersonal: the truth layer, the reserve, the assets, the structure, the rooms, run for everyone and exempt no one, no matter the title on the badge or the name on the building. I watched brilliant people at brilliant institutions learn this the expensive way, and the lesson was never that the institutions were villains. The lesson was that the program was always the individual's to run, and the badge had quietly convinced them otherwise.

THE OFFICE RAT AND THE OWNER

Not a job status. A posture. Both can collect a W-2.

THE OFFICE RAT	THE OWNER
Waits for permission	Moves without permission
Optimizes for approval	Optimizes for equity
Performs effort for managers	Produces results, not visibility
Ratmaxxing: busy theater	Builds the gap and the skills
Calls a pay raise a plan	Runs C.A.T. on the whole year
Builds nothing that belongs to him	Owns what earns without his hours

Every hour spent performing for the org chart is an hour not spent on the gap, the skills, or the rooms.

BEFORE 40 CLUB

The Office Rat and the Owner: two postures, one choice

One clarification before the audit, because ownership is bigger than owning a business. The Owner posture extends to the whole operation: the Owner books the medical appointments, chooses the food, gets the daily movement, protects the sleep, curates the environment, guards the energy, runs the calendar, tends the relationships, and makes the financial decisions, all without waiting. The Office Rat waits, for the health scare, the job loss, the birthday, the breakup, the crisis, to grant permission for action. The Owner does not need the emergency, because the Owner already has the calendar.

The C.A.T. Breakdown

C: The Owner runs personal cash flow like corporate finance: the paycheck is revenue, the lifestyle is operating expense, the gap is retained earnings, and retained earnings get deployed, never merely accumulated. The Office Rat's cash flow tell is the opposite posture: one hundred percent of income from one payer, one hundred percent of the gap unassigned, and a raise strategy that consists entirely of hoping. Run your household like the CFO would run it if your life were a company, because it is one, and you are the only officer it will ever have.

A: The career itself is the first asset under management, and the Owner manages it like Chapter 5 manages everything: the skill stack invested in deliberately, the reputation compounding in rooms per Chapter 17, the market price tested per Chapter 16, and, always, the conversion question running: what am I building that survives this job? The Office Rat's asset column is the tell that hurts most: decades of excellence, all of it accruing to someone else's balance sheet, none of it converted, hours sold at wholesale with nothing owned at retail. Excellence is not the issue. Ownership of the excellence is.

T: The posture shows up on the return, and after eighteen years I can read it in thirty seconds: the Office Rat's return is one W-2, standard deduction, default withholding, no entity, no planning, the tax life of a person things happen to. The Owner's return grows texture over the quarters: the side income with its Schedule C, then the entity, the owner retirement accounts, the planned timing, the professional's fingerprints, the tax life of a person who happens to things. Chapter 6 gave you the whole playbook, and this chapter adds the diagnosis: your return is not just a scoreboard of your money. It is a posture report. Pull yours and read which person filed it.

The Quarter Lens

Q2: The posture-setting quarter, and the most dangerous decade to Ratmaxx, because the theater feels like investment: the face time, the politics, the performing, all of it plausible as career-building while the actual assets, skills, gap, engine, rooms, go unbuilt. The Q2 Owner extracts everything the job offers, skills, proof, network, capital, and builds nights and weekends. Q2 decides which person sits at the Q3 desk.

Q3: The divergence quarter, where the postures finish compounding and the results stop being subtle. The Q3 Owner has options: the business at scale, or the career priced at peak with assets beside it, and every negotiation backstopped by the ability to walk. The Q3 Office Rat has tenure and terror: peak lifestyle, single payer, no engine, and the first cold breeze of age discrimination in an industry he assumed was family. Q3 is also the last cheap exit: the bridge can still be built at 45, but the toll rises every year.

Q4: The audit arrives for everyone. The Owner's Q4 is a choice among goods: sell, scale down, advise, continue by preference. The Office Rat's Q4 is arithmetic performed by others: the package, the pension math, the discovery that the institution's memory of his loyalty is shorter than his mortgage. The kindest thing this chapter can do is make that paragraph avoidable, and it is, entirely, in Q2 and Q3.

Overtime: Titles evaporate at retirement parties. What transfers is what was owned: the assets, the business, the name, the rooms, the posture itself, modeled for children who watched. Nobody inherits a badge. Chapter 13 and the close of this book carry it from here.

The Move to Make Now

One audit, one reallocation, one build, thirty days.

The posture audit, this week, on paper, brutal: last month's hours sorted into three columns, building what I own, serving the client excellently, and performing for approval. The third column is your Ratmaxxing number, and it is about to become your reallocation budget. Then the dependency check: what percentage of income comes from one payer, what happens in month one, three, and six if it stops, and does the answer describe a company you would invest in?

The reallocation, next week: cut the performance column in half, hold the excellence column steady, because the client deserves the excellence and the reputation feeds Chapter 17, and move the recovered hours, explicitly, on the calendar, to the build: the skill from Chapter 16, the engine, the rooms.

The build, this month: if the engine from Chapter 16 exists, give it the structure Chapter 10 demands. If it does not, write its thesis and take the first customer-facing step, the offer made, the first dollar sought, because the Owner's posture is proven in revenue, not intention. And if leaving is genuinely on your horizon: open the four-gates document today, reserve, revenue, structure, tax, with honest numbers next to each, and let the gates, not the mood after a bad meeting, set the date.

The Warning

Two misreadings of this chapter will cost people money, so let me close both doors.

The first: this chapter is not anti-employment, and the Owner posture is not a resignation letter. Some of the wealthiest, freest people I serve are career employees who ran the program flawlessly: priced their work like Chapter 16, converted income to assets like Chapter 5, kept single-payer risk hedged, and treated the institution as an excellent client for thirty years. The W-2 is a tool. The waiting is the trap. Do not confuse the paper with the posture.

The second: agency without the program is just the Goofball with a manifesto. The person who reads this chapter, feels the fire, and torches the job with three weeks of reserve and a logo has not escaped the Office Rat, he has funded a more expensive costume, and Chapter 20 has a seat saved for him. Urgency means the quarters are running. Agency means you move without permission. The program means you move in order: truth layer, reserve, engine, structure, bridge. All three words, together, every time. Nobody cares more than you will, nobody is coming, and no one, at any desk, in any posture, is bigger than the program.

The Checklist

☐ Complete the posture audit: last month's hours in three columns, Ratmaxxing number named

☐ Run the dependency check: single-payer percentage and the one, three, six month answer

☐ Cut the performance column in half; calendar the recovered hours to the build

☐ Reframe in writing: the employer as largest client, the paycheck as runway

☐ Extract deliberately: list what the current job funds, skills, rooms, proof, and use them on purpose

The Before 40 Club Rule

Nobody is coming to promote you into your own life. Same desk, two postures, two futures. Move like the Owner, in order, starting now.

One question before you go. Which posture did I bring to my desk this week, the Rat or the Owner?

Agency: Which column of your hours, results, performance, or building, do you control most directly? **Urgency:** Which Ratmaxxing behavior retires this week, and where do the hours go?

Put this chapter to work in the companion Before 40 Club Workbook at before40club.com.

CHAPTER 19:

THE BUILDER: FROM PATTERNS TO PLATFORMS

"Build the market while you build the product."

The Expensive Lesson

Everybody in your feed has information. Almost nobody has judgment, and judgment is the only one of the two that gets paid.

Here is the progression, and I want you to find yourself on it honestly. Facts answer what is true. Patterns answer what keeps happening. Insights answer why it keeps happening. Strategy answers what to do about it. Execution answers how to make it happen. Many people collect facts. Fewer recognize patterns. Even fewer connect those patterns into strategies, and a tiny group actually executes. Every step up that ladder, the crowd thins and the pay rises, because the market prices scarcity, and at the top of that ladder scarcity is absolute.

This chapter is the story of climbing it, told through the two companies I built, because I want you to see the ladder in a real life and not a diagram. I spent years reading tax returns, thousands of them, and returns are pattern data of the purest kind. The same confusions, the same questions, the same expensive mistakes, arriving at my desk in different bodies. A fact collector sees a thousand returns. A pattern recognizer sees one return, a thousand times. The day I understood that difference was the day I stopped being only an accountant and started being a builder, and everything with my name on it since, the firm, the software, this book, came out of that single shift.

The expensive lesson: your industry is showing you its patterns right now, every day, for free, and almost everyone you work with is deleting that data as noise. Seeing the relationships between facts, connecting the dots into a picture that makes decisions better, is the whole difference between a career and a platform. Intelligence was never about knowing more facts.

The Story

The whole arc starts with a pattern I did not plan. At Fordham I had my real estate license, because I always wanted something in business, and it was that license, in a chance encounter, that opened the conversation which turned into an internship in the tax department at Ernst and Young. Get around strangers was working on my life before I had the letters for it. One credential I picked up for one dream unlocked a completely different door, which taught me early that you cannot predict which preparation pays, you can only keep preparing.

AskMyUncleSam came from a tally. I always kept CPA clients on the side, and the same messages kept arriving: hey Busayo, can I deduct this, can I do that, what about this. The same questions, over and over, from different people, and one night at Five Oaks the pattern crossed the threshold: if I could build a repository of those questions and answers, I could turn the conversation into a product. I even had the operating model already proven, because at my own firm I routed work to contractors, so I knew a system could deliver what a person used to. And when Techstars came around in 2022, the decision was a mindset before it was a strategy: refuse the story that you are too old for the room. I look at entrepreneurship as reps. You do not know what you do not know, and the only cure is the next repetition. This book is a repetition too, 18 years and thousands of returns, stepped back from thirty thousand feet: below, I see what I see.

The public record of that arc is simple enough to state. In December 2016 I founded AMUS and built AskMyUncleSam, an AI chatbot that answered tax questions, aimed at the two hundred forty three million Americans who file. Facebook's FbStart program backed it with forty thousand dollars in credits. VentureBeat and CoinDesk covered it. Queen City Fintech selected it for their accelerator out of more than a hundred companies from twenty countries. And in 2022 I co-founded Muse Tax, a Techstars company, a B2B platform that delivers tax and financial insights through an API to payroll companies, banks, and credit agencies. Every one of those sentences is a fact. The pattern underneath them is the actual chapter.

What Nobody Told You

Nobody told you the difference between information and judgment

Information is abundant, which means information is cheap. The tax code is public. Every strategy in this book is discoverable. What is scarce is the climb: facts to patterns to insights to strategy to execution, and the market pays at every rung for exactly one reason: fewer people are standing on it. This is why two professionals with the same credential bill numbers an order of magnitude apart. One sells facts. The other sells judgment, which is pattern recognition with a track record. Whatever field you are in, your raw pattern data is flowing past you today. The builder's first act is refusing to delete it.

Nobody told you that pattern recognition is a trade you can practice

It is not a gift. It is a habit with a notebook. For an entrepreneur, it looks like this: seeing a customer complaint and recognizing a business opportunity. Seeing an IRS notice and envisioning an entire workflow platform instead of a scary document. Seeing content, software, partnerships, and distribution as parts of one flywheel instead of separate projects. My version was concrete: the same twelve tax questions kept walking through the door of a New York tax practice, which meant millions of people were asking those questions everywhere, which meant the answers could be a product instead of a conversation. AskMyUncleSam was not a stroke of genius. It was a tally mark that got long enough to act on. Start the tally. Ask weekly: what keeps happening in front of me that everyone treats as noise?

Nobody told you that distribution is the moat

Here is the mental model that took me two companies to earn. Product answers: what do you sell? Workflow answers: when and how is it used? Distribution answers: how do customers find it? And embedded distribution answers the richest question of all: how can customers receive it as part of something they are already doing? Customer acquisition is usually the most expensive part of building anything. If your product becomes a natural step inside another organization's workflow, every additional customer gets cheaper, which is why Muse does not sell tax insights to millions of small businesses one at a time. It delivers them through the payroll companies, banks, and credit agencies those businesses already use. The formula, and it is worth memorizing: pattern recognition leads to a repeatable workflow, the workflow earns embedded distribution, distribution produces recurring revenue, revenue generates proprietary data, and the data makes the product stronger. That loop is the moat. Products get copied. Distribution compounds. And this is not just a startup lesson: this book you are holding is embedded distribution for a firm, and your expertise, whatever it is, has a distribution question waiting to be asked.

Nobody told you to work with the willing

The most expensive customers, partners, and even family members are the ones you have to drag. Early in anything, the temptation is to chase the skeptic, to win the argument, to convert the person with folded arms, because conversion feels like validation. It is actually the highest customer acquisition cost you will ever pay, billed in energy instead of dollars. The willing are already in motion: the client who wants the plan and not just the refund, the partner who answers the first email, the early adopter who forgives the rough edges because they need the thing. Build with them, sell to them, learn from them, and let the skeptics arrive later, in the audience, where they belong. This rule runs everywhere in the club: Chapter 13 taught it about family money, Chapter 17 taught it about rooms, and the builder learns it about markets. Willingness is the qualification. Everything else is teachable.

Nobody told you that the credential does not exempt you from shipping

I was a CPA with elite-institution experience and a Master of Science in Taxation, and none of it wrote a line of the chatbot, filled out the accelerator application, or survived the first demo that went sideways. Expertise is the raw material of pattern recognition, and it is also the world's most comfortable place to hide, because researching, credentialing, and preparing all feel like progress and risk nothing. Chapter 5 called this the researcher. The builder's version of the cure is the same: the smallest real version, shipped to the willing, this quarter. Two hundred forty three million people file taxes. My first version served a handful of them badly, and that handful taught me more than the credential ever did.

And nobody told you the day job funds the build

The dates in my own record tell this one: AMUS and the tax practice were founded in December 2016, and I did not leave the controller desk until October 2017. Ten months of W-2 by day and founder by night, exactly the Owner posture from the last chapter, the employer as largest client, the paycheck as runway. I am not romanticizing the season. I am reporting the sequence, because the leap everyone glamorizes was actually a bridge, engineered from cash flow, reserves, and a boring calendar. Builders who burn the boats make better movies. Builders who build the bridge make better companies.

The C.A.T. Breakdown

C: The build is funded by the gap, full stop. Product experiments, accelerator travel, the months of ramen revenue: all of it draws on the cash flow discipline of Chapter 4, which is why the truth layer comes before the dream in this book's order. And the build inherits the same rules: a budget line with a number, a runway measured in months and known cold, and the reserve untouched, because a founder without a reserve does not make decisions, he makes gambles.

A: A platform is the purest asset in this book: it earns without your hours, it compounds through data, and it can outlive you. But the A discipline cuts both ways. The equity clocks from Chapter 15, the 83(b), the QSBS window, the papered co-founder vesting, all started ticking for me at formation, and the CPA in the founder chair had to run his own playbook. If you build, your company is your largest asset and it deserves the same one-page thesis, the same real math, and the same paperwork discipline as any rental or portfolio.

T: Builders live inside the richest and most unforgiving corner of the tax code. The entity chosen at formation decides the exit's tax treatment years later. The R&D and startup cost rules, the accelerator stipends, the SAFE conversions, all land somewhere on a return. And the boring foundation from Chapter 10, clean books, no mixing, a reserve, the estimated rhythm, is what lets a builder take every legal advantage without fear. The code rewards owners, and it rewards documented owners most of all.

The Quarter Lens

Q1 (0 to 21): The tally habit installs early. A young person who writes down what keeps happening around them is running builder software before they have anything to build.

Q2 (21 to 40): The building quarter, and the bridge quarter. Energy is high, obligations are lighter, mistakes are recoverable, and the day job can fund the night build. Both of my companies were conceived in Q2. If you are in Q2 with a pattern in your notebook, the cost of the smallest real version will never be lower.

Q3 (41 to 60): The judgment quarter. Q3 builders trade raw hours for pattern libraries no younger founder can match, which is why the accelerator cohort should not scare you. Twenty years of watching an industry is a moat that cannot be raised.

Q4 (61 to 80): The platform harvest, or the platform sale, run on the exit structures decided decades earlier, and the mentorship years, where your pattern library becomes other people's shortcut.

Overtime: A platform that runs without you is the only business that attends your legacy instead of your calendar.

The Move to Make Now

Open a note on your phone and title it the tally. For the next thirty days, log every repeated thing your work shows you: the question clients keep asking, the complaint customers keep filing, the manual step everyone keeps doing, the document everyone keeps fearing. One line each, no analysis. On day thirty, read the list and circle the pattern with the most tally marks, then write four sentences about it: what I sell (product), when and how it is used (workflow), how customers find it (distribution), and how customers could receive it inside something they already do (embedded distribution). You now hold a one-page platform thesis, built from your own pattern data, and the next move is Chapter 16's: the smallest priced version, offered to the willing, this quarter.

The Warning

The warning is the flywheel that never spins. Pattern recognition without execution curdles into something worse than ignorance: the person at every dinner who saw it coming, called it early, and built nothing, collecting patterns the way the researcher collects articles, as a costume of progress. The ladder in this chapter ends at execution on purpose, because every rung below it pays nothing on its own. And the second warning is the mirror of the first: shipping without patterns, the serial launcher chasing whatever is loud this quarter, burning the gap on products nobody's tally justified. The tally without the ship is a diary. The ship without the tally is a lottery ticket. The builder is the discipline of doing both, in order, on a calendar.

The Checklist

☐ Start the tally note today and log repeated patterns for thirty days

☐ On day thirty: circle the strongest pattern and write the four sentences, product, workflow, distribution, embedded distribution

☐ Memorize the formula: pattern to workflow to embedded distribution to recurring revenue to proprietary data to stronger product

☐ Identify your willing: the five people already in motion who would use the smallest version

☐ Price the smallest real version and offer it to the willing this quarter

The Before 40 Club Rule

Facts are free. Judgment gets paid. See the pattern, build the workflow, embed the distribution, and work with the willing.

One question before you go. What keeps happening in front of me that everyone else deletes as noise?

Put this chapter to work in the companion Before 40 Club Workbook at before40club.com.

CHAPTER 20:

THE GOOFBALL CHAPTER

"I do not worry about what other people do. I live and do me."

The Expensive Lesson

Every finance book has a chapter the author skipped. This is that chapter, and I refuse to skip it.

Here is the lesson: your biggest financial losses will not come from the market, the IRS, or the economy. They will come from you, being a goofball, in ways that felt completely reasonable at the time. The wrong friends kept too long. The partner you never had the money conversation with. The co-founder you chose on chemistry instead of alignment. The ego purchases. The oversharing that armed people with a map to your pockets. The years spent performing success for people who were not paying your bills and never would.

I can teach you the tax code all day. But the tax code never cost anyone what a misaligned person cost them. A misaligned person is an expensive liability, and unlike a bad stock, they do not show up on any statement. They show up in your decisions, your stress, your delays, and eventually your bank account, and by the time you total the damage, it has been compounding for years.

The financial industry pretends money mistakes are math mistakes. They are not. They are mostly people mistakes and ego mistakes wearing a math costume. So before this book ends, we are going to sit in the uncomfortable chair and talk about the goofball. Mine first.

The Story

Three scars, told in the order I earned them.

The wrong circle first. In my past life there were people around me who did not value my time, my money, my ideas, my network, or my business acumen, and for too long I let them keep their access anyway, because access felt like loyalty and reassessing it felt like betrayal. Here is the reframe that fixed it. Look at how the people at the top actually operate: Warren Buffett auctions a single dinner once a year. You cannot simply get LeBron James or Michael Rubin on the phone. The most successful people on earth are deliberately not easily accessible, while staying wide open to real opportunity, and that is not arrogance, it is architecture. I was fortunate in one respect: I played college football at Fordham, and many of those teammates grew into founders, owners, and CPAs, so I had a picture of what an aligned circle looked like. The rule I eventually installed is the one I now hand to every client: I know what my time costs per hour, so what is the ROI of this relationship? People can be aligned for a season of your life and wrong for the next quarter of it, and if a relationship is costing you sleep, energy, and progress on your C.A.T., the most expensive currency it is billing you in is time, the only one with no refund policy.

The ego second, and I will tell it on myself. When the firm started producing real cash flow, twenty to fifty thousand dollars a month in profits, fresh out of corporate, I did what almost everyone does with a level of freedom they have never held before: I took the trips. I spent the money. And the education arrived the moment I got around established entrepreneurs earning the same numbers, because standing next to them I realized, in the exact words I used on myself, that I was low key a loser, because every one of those dollars could have been doubled down, poured into the ads, the growth, the machine, and I had converted growth capital into consumption instead. The checks I now run before any money leaves, and the ones I am handing you: what is coming in next month, is the retirement capital funded, are the tax reserves full. Only then does lifestyle get a vote.

The misalignment third. The lesson that took longest: you cannot over-index people, because you do not actually know anyone's skill set, work habits, or operating standards until you are up close, and two people can read the same books and carry completely different levels of urgency and agency. So I built a filter for partners and collaborators, and it sounds trivial until it saves you: do we work well under pressure, and are our standards aligned? I fly business or first. If a potential partner shrugs and says coach is fine, that is not a seating preference, it is data, because how you do everything is how you do everything, and a person with a five-star expectation of life runs a five-star standard everywhere. Choosing a business partner is a marriage, and it deserves the same diligence Chapter 7 demands of one: the work habits, the thought process, the family patterns, the vision of their own life, examined before anything is signed. The music business gave everyone the famous version of this lesson: two men built the same label, and the roads out of it went in two very different directions, because a partnership aligned for a season is not the same as a partnership aligned for the build.

Add it all up across ten years and the goofball's bill is not one number, it is a route: delayed opportunities, delayed transactions, networks never entered, even the timeline to meeting a life partner, because when you are not on track to where you want to be, everything downstream waits too. I call it the long way home, and the long way home is just a life full of extra detours. Here is the uncomfortable truth about that path: it is crowded on purpose, because nobody hands out the ideas and the structures, and the defaults are designed for the many. The exits are the chapters you have already read, get around strangers, make more money, protect the revenue generating hours, and I am telling you my detours for one reason: so you can recognize the on-ramps before you take them.

Notice the pattern across every story I just told you. Not one of them was a math failure. I could always do the math. Every single one was a judgment failure, an access failure, or an ego failure. The math was fine. The goofball was in charge.

What Nobody Told You

Nobody told you that your friends do not need access to your money to cost you money

They cost you through your calendar, your standards, and your defaults. The circle that mocks the budget, that treats every payday as an event, that measures each other in purchases, will tax you more reliably than any government, and there is no deduction for it. You do not have to catch anyone stealing. The environment does the stealing, slowly, with your full cooperation.

Nobody told you that oversharing is a financial risk

When you were broke, telling everyone your business cost nothing, because there was nothing to map. The moment you start building, information about your money becomes a map to it. Announce the windfall and watch the asks arrive. Detail the business and watch opinions, jealousy, and hands appear. Privacy is not paranoia. Privacy is an asset-protection strategy that costs nothing and is broken most often by your own mouth.

Nobody told you that ego has a billing department

Ego spends money to answer questions nobody asked. It buys the car for people at red lights, the bottle for the section, the office before the revenue, the upgrade that turned one good year into a permanent overhead. Ratmaxxing is the corporate version, performing urgency and success for an audience of managers, but there is a street version too: optimizing your money for applause. Every ego dollar is a double loss. You lose the dollar, and you lose everything the dollar would have become inside the C.A.T. loop.

Nobody told you that misalignment is measured in dollars, eventually

The partner who spends against your saving. The co-founder who wants a lifestyle while you want an exit. The client who disrespects the scope. The hire who needed managing harder than the work itself. At first, misalignment reads as friction, personality, vibes. Give it time and it converts, reliably, into money: deals delayed, splits litigated, businesses stalled, decades of compounding forfeited. You do not have a personality conflict. You have an unpriced liability.

And nobody told you the goofball never fully retires

He is not a phase. He is a passenger. He rides along for life, and he gets louder exactly when things go well, because success is his favorite disguise. The goal of this chapter is not to kill him. You cannot. The goal is to take his hands off the wheel and never give them back.

So you can recognize him, here are his five favorite faces. You have worn at least two. I have worn more.

The Flexer. Spends to be perceived. The car for strangers, the trip for the feed, the watch that answers a question nobody asked. The Flexer's tell is that the purchase needs an audience to make sense. Alone in a room, he would never buy it.

The Loyalist. Funds people out of history instead of judgment. Lends to the childhood friend because of who they were at 19, not who they are at 34. Cannot say no to family, so his money says yes for him, over and over, and calls it love. The Loyalist's tell is the phrase, I could not say no. You could. It just cost comfort, and he preferred to pay cash.

The Genius. Too smart for the boring play. Skips the reserve, the index, the plan, because he found an angle, a loophole, a guy. The Genius does not lose money on bad luck. He loses it on complexity he chose over discipline. His tell is contempt for anything that works slowly.

The Avoider. Does not open the letter. Does not have the conversation. Does not look at the return, the statement, or the partner's spending, because looking makes it real. The Avoider believes silence pauses the game. The game does not pause. It compounds against him quietly, and the invoice arrives with penalties and interest. His tell is the word later.

The Broadcaster. Cannot build in silence. Announces the deal before it closes, the number before it clears, the plan before it starts. Every announcement recruits opinions, envy, and asks. The Broadcaster's tell is that everyone in his life knows his business and somehow nobody in his life is helping it.

Five faces, one passenger. Name the ones you wear, because you cannot bench a player you refuse to identify.

The Goofball Filter: expand aggressively, admit selectively

The C.A.T. Breakdown

Run the goofball through the method and watch how much damage one clown does to all three letters.

C: The goofball attacks cash flow through lifestyle and circle. Every upgrade he normalizes becomes permanent overhead. Every yes to the environment widens the out and shrinks the gap, and the gap, remember, is your entire future in one number. The goofball does not blow up your budget in a day. He renegotiates it downward, monthly, forever.

A: The goofball buys costumes and calls them assets. He is also the reason people fund friends instead of buying assets, chase status deals instead of boring cash flow, and hand equity to misaligned partners because the conversation felt awkward. Awkward conversations are cheap. Their absence is not. The most expensive asset mistakes I have ever seen were relationship decisions wearing an investment costume.

T: The goofball ignores letters because they are scary, skips the reserve because this year is different, takes internet loopholes because they flatter him, and does not keep records because records are for later. Then later arrives with interest and penalties. Almost every tax disaster on my desk in 18 years had a goofball decision at the root of it, usually made years earlier, usually in about four seconds.

The Quarter Lens

Q2 (21 to 40) is the goofball's home stadium. Maximum energy, maximum ego, minimum evidence, and enough income to arm all three. Most of the tuition in this chapter gets paid in Q2, which is exactly why the Before 40 Club exists. Every goofball dollar in Q2 is a compounding machine you set on fire.

Q3 (41 to 60) upgrades his taste. Fewer bottles, bigger mistakes: the vanity business, the misaligned partnership entered at scale, the lifestyle locked in at peak earnings that becomes a cage the moment earnings dip.

Q4 and Overtime are where his old bills come due and his new tricks get darker: the adult child funded into permanent dependence, the pressure decision, the scheme pitched by a familiar face to someone who stopped getting around new information years ago. The goofball you do not confront in Q2 negotiates your Q4.

Purpose comes first, in every quarter, and that is the real defense. A person with a defined purpose has a filter. Every dollar either serves the purpose or it does not. The goofball cannot operate through a filter like that. He needs vagueness to work.

The Move to Make Now

Do the audit nobody wants to do. Tonight, on paper, three lists.

List one: the goofball ledger. Every significant loss of the last ten years that was not math. The people, the purchases, the partnerships, the silence, the oversharing. Next to each, the honest dollar figure, including what the money would have become by now inside the loop. Do not perform shame. Just total it. That number is your personal tuition receipt, and you should know it the way you know your salary.

List two: current access. Every person who currently has access to your money, your decisions, or your detailed financial information. Next to each name, one word: aligned or misaligned. You already know. You have known for a while.

List three: the open conversations. Every money conversation you have been avoiding, with a partner, a friend you funded, a co-founder, a family member. Pick the single most expensive silence on the list and schedule the conversation within seven days. Awkward is the fee. Freedom is what it buys.

The Warning

The trap in a chapter like this is reading it about other people. You will catch yourself doing it, nodding along, thinking of your cousin, your old business partner, that guy from the job. Stop. This chapter is a mirror, not a window. Nobody cares more than you will, and that includes caring enough to look at your own receipts without flinching.

And one more warning, because I love you enough to say it: do not weaponize this chapter into paranoia. The answer to the wrong circle is not no circle. It is a better one. GAS still stands. Get around strangers, better rooms, people building what you are building. The goal was never isolation. The goal is curation. Misaligned people cost money. Aligned people make you money in ways no spreadsheet predicts. Choose rooms accordingly.

The Checklist

☐ Write the goofball ledger and total your ten-year tuition, honestly

☐ List everyone with access to your money, decisions, or financial details, and mark each: aligned or misaligned

☐ Identify your single most expensive avoided conversation and schedule it within 7 days

☐ Find the last ego purchase still costing you monthly, and cancel, sell, or downgrade it

☐ Set a personal information rule: who gets numbers, who gets headlines, who gets nothing

The Before 40 Club Rule

The goofball rides for life. Your job is not to kill him. Your job is to make sure he never drives again.

One question before you go. Who in my circle makes me spend, doubt, or perform?

Put this chapter to work in the companion Before 40 Club Workbook at before40club.com.

PART IV:
THE ENDGAME

Three chapters and the final whistle: retirement, the estate, and the ninety days that install everything. This is where the whole system points, the quarter everything else was quietly funding, and the plan that makes the book permanent.

CHAPTER 21:

RETIREMENT: THE HOPE PLAN AND THE C.A.T. PLAN

"You cannot retire by 40 while still carrying decisions from your twenties."

The Expensive Lesson

Ask people about their retirement plan and most of them will describe a feeling.

It will be fine. The 401k is doing something. Social Security will be there, probably. The house will be paid off, maybe. We will figure it out when we get closer. I call this the Hope Plan, and it is the single most popular retirement strategy in America. It requires no math, no documents, and no decisions, which is exactly why it is so popular and exactly why it fails. Hope is not a plan. Hope is what people call the absence of one when they need to change the subject.

Here is the eighteen-year pattern from my chair. The people who retire well are not the people who earned the most. They are the people who converted earnings into assets that pay for life without hours, and who protected those assets from the six wreckers this chapter will name. The people who retire scared earned plenty. They just ran the Hope Plan through Q2 and Q3, and by the time hope files for retirement, the compounding years are gone and no amount of Q4 effort buys them back.

So this chapter replaces the feeling with a definition. Retirement is not an age. Retirement is a math event: the day your assets can pay for your life at your real monthly cost, permanently, without your hours. Some people hit that math at 50. Some never hit it at 75. The difference is not luck. It is whether they ran the Hope Plan or the C.A.T. Plan, and you get to choose which one today, in Q2 or Q3, while the choice is still cheap.

The Story

Clients arrive at my desk in every quarter of life, and the two retirements look exactly like this. A client came to me near sixty with a strong salary history and a plan made entirely of hope, and I will be honest about that meeting: it was scary, for both of us, because at sixty you do not have the vitality and the vigor you are silently counting on, and the compounding years are not for sale at any price. Here is the math I want tattooed on every reader in Q2: when you hit forty, you have roughly fifteen prime working years to fifty-five. If the game plan was not run in Q1 and Q2, picking up assets later in life gets brutally hard.

Against him, another client, and his file is one of my favorites in eighteen years: he bought an investment property nearly every quarter for five to seven years, Ohio, Tampa, the Midwest, nothing glamorous, just the boring repetition. By Q3 he held seven properties quietly paying for his life, and retirement for him is not a hope, it is an arithmetic result. And then the wreckers, which I watch operate in real time: clients in their fifties and sixties in gray divorces right now, selling the prized possessions, splitting the primary residence, the retirement accounts, even the pets. Clients in their sixties still carrying Parent PLUS loans they signed for their children. And the health scares that can consume a decade of savings in one season. This is why I harp on C.A.T. with the intensity I do: enough cash flow, enough assets, and enough tax planning is the difference between protected and exposed, and you choose which one decades before you find out.

Every version of that contrast has the same root. One person treated retirement as a distant event that would somehow organize itself. The other treated it as a number with a deadline and worked the number. The number is not complicated. It is just relentless, and it only responds to decades.

What Nobody Told You

Nobody told you what retirement actually is

It is not a party, an age, or a government program. It is the day work becomes optional because assets cover the true monthly cost of your life. Which means retirement is not a Q4 topic. It is a Q2 and Q3 construction project, and every chapter of this book has secretly been about it: the gap funds it, the assets are it, and tax planning protects it. If you have been doing the work since Chapter 4, you have been building retirement this whole time. This chapter just puts a roof on it.

Nobody told you the Hope Plan has a default outcome, and you have already seen it

The Hope Plan ends in one of three places: working past 70 not by choice, a sharp downgrade in lifestyle managed with dignity but felt every day, or becoming a line in an adult child's budget. That third one deserves a hard look, because Chapter 13 already showed you what family financial rescue does to both sides of it. The greatest gift you will ever hand your children is not an inheritance. It is a retirement that never calls them.

Nobody told you the C.A.T. Plan is just a number with a date

Here is the whole method. Take your true monthly cost from Chapter 4 and multiply by twelve: that is the annual price of your life. Retirement is funded when your assets can produce that number every year without being spent to zero. A rough gauge the industry uses: total assets of roughly twenty-five times your annual cost puts a sustainable withdrawal in reach. Income-producing assets, the rentals, the business, the dividends, count double in comfort because they pay without being sold. You do not need the gauge to be perfect. You need a number on paper, a date next to it, and a monthly contribution that connects today to it. Vague retirements never arrive. Numbered ones do.

Nobody told you the accounts are tax containers, and the mix decides your Q4 bill

Pre-tax accounts, the traditional 401k and IRA, give you the deduction now and hand you a partner later, because every dollar in them is taxed on the way out and required minimum distributions eventually force the dollars out on the government's schedule, not yours. Roth accounts take the tax hit now and pay out clean forever. Taxable accounts fill the space between. A retirement built entirely pre-tax is a retirement with the IRS listed as a silent partner, and the drawdown sequencing from Chapter 6, which account gets touched first and when, routinely swings six figures across a retirement. This is a June conversation with your strategist, decades early. It is barely a conversation at all in April of your first retired year.

Nobody told you about the six wreckers

Retirement is rarely killed by markets. It is killed by liens on your cash flow and cuts to your assets, and they have names. Student loans, yours or the Parent PLUS loans you signed for the kids, following you into your sixties, because education debt survives almost everything and the oxygen mask rule from Chapter 9 exists precisely for this. Divorce, especially gray divorce, which splits in one afternoon the assets two people spent thirty years building, and runs both households on money sized for one. Taxes, the quiet wrecker, taking their share of every unplanned withdrawal and every forced distribution. Child support and alimony, which are court-ordered cash flow commitments that do not care what your retirement date was. And bad health, the biggest of them all, because a single uninsured season can consume a decade of compounding, which is why health insurance without gaps, disability insurance while you are still earning, and the HSA, the only account in the code that is deductible going in, untaxed growing, and untaxed coming out for medical costs, are retirement strategies wearing insurance costumes. You cannot prevent every wrecker. You can price them, insure against the insurable ones, and refuse to sign for the voluntary ones.

Nobody told you about the bill Medicare does not cover

The largest health wrecker has its own name: long-term care, the years of assistance with daily living that ordinary health insurance and Medicare largely do not pay for, and that can consume in a few years what took decades to build. There are four honest answers to it, and the only wrong move is not choosing one. You can self-insure, if the asset base is genuinely large enough to absorb a multi-year care bill without breaking the surviving spouse's retirement. You can buy long-term care insurance, traditional or the newer hybrid policies that pair the coverage with life insurance, and the pricing rule is unforgiving: this is a decision for your fifties, while you are healthy enough to qualify and young enough that the premiums make sense, not a Q4 purchase made after the diagnosis. You can plan around it structurally, which is the irrevocable trust conversation from the next chapter, done years ahead because the calendar is the entire trick. Or you can default, which quietly elects your children's savings as the policy. Price the four options in Q3 with your strategist, choose on paper, and this wrecker loses most of its power.

And nobody told you that Social Security is a floor, not a plan

It will likely exist for you in some form, it will not resemble a salary, and the age you claim it changes the check for the rest of your life. Treat it as the concrete under the building, never the building.

The C.A.T. Breakdown

C: Retirement is a cash flow question wearing a savings costume. The real question is never how big is the pile, it is what does my life cost per month and what pays that bill when hours stop. Run the truth layer on your future: today's true monthly cost, adjusted honestly for the life you actually intend, is the target your assets must fund. And the contribution that builds it lives inside the gap, automated, dated the day after payday, exactly like Chapter 4 taught, because retirement is just the gap with a fifty-year job description.

A: The retirement is the asset portfolio. The accounts, the funds inside them, the real estate, the business equity, all of Chapter 5 pointed here. The A discipline now is allocation across tax containers, pre-tax, Roth, taxable, and the double-comfort of income-producing assets that pay without being sold. One warning from the desk: your primary home is shelter, not retirement, unless you have a written plan to convert it, downsize it, or rent it. Equity you will never access is a number on a statement, not a monthly check.

T: Q2 and Q3 tax planning decides the Q4 tax bill. The container mix, the Roth conversions run deliberately in lower-income years, the drawdown order, the RMD plan made a decade before RMDs exist, the HSA funded and invested rather than spent, and for owners, the retirement plans with owner-sized ceilings from Chapter 10. Every one of those is a during-the-year move with a December 31 expiration, and stacked across twenty years they are frequently worth more than the investment returns people obsess over.

The Quarter Lens

Q1 (0 to 21): Nobody retires in Q1, but retirements are installed here. A teenager with earned income and a custodial Roth, from Chapter 9, owns the longest runway in the entire code.

Q2 (21 to 40): The quarter that decides everything. A dollar automated at 30 outworks several dollars panicked at 50, and the habits, the containers, and the contribution rate installed here are the whole ballgame. If you are in Q2, the C.A.T. Plan costs you a worksheet and an automation. That is the entire price of not becoming the 62-year-old with a feeling.

Q3 (41 to 60): The catch-up quarter, literally, the code allows larger contributions at 50 and beyond, and the quarter where the wreckers circle hardest: the divorces, the Parent PLUS temptations, the health surprises. Q3 with a numbered plan is acceleration. Q3 with a feeling is the last exit before the Hope Plan's default outcome.

Q4 (61 to 80): The harvest, run on sequencing. Which account first, when to claim the floor, how the brackets get managed. Q4 executed with structure is calm. Q4 improvised is a tax bill with a view.

Overtime: What remains transfers, which is the next chapter's entire job.

The Move to Make Now

One page, this week. At the top: my true monthly cost times twelve. That is the annual price of your life. Multiply by twenty-five: that is the gauge. Under it, list every current retirement asset by tax container: pre-tax, Roth, taxable, and what each is worth today. Subtract. The distance between the gauge and the total is not bad news. It is the assignment, and it divides by the months you have left in Q2 and Q3 into a monthly number. Automate that number, or the honest fraction of it you can start with, dated the day after payday, this week. Then name your wreckers in writing: every loan you have cosigned or are tempted to, the insurance gaps, the court-ordered commitments, the health coverage status. A wrecker named is a wrecker priced. Sixty minutes, one page, and you have replaced a feeling with a plan.

The Warning

The warning is the word later. Retirement is the most postponable project in your financial life because the deadline is decades out and the penalty for skipping this month is invisible. That is exactly how the Hope Plan recruits: one skipped month at a time, each individually harmless, thirty years in a row. The math does not punish you today. It punishes you all at once, at 62, in a meeting I have sat in many times, and I can tell you the feeling in that room is not regret about markets. It is regret about months. Do not donate your months to later. Later is not on your side. Compounding is, but only if you feed it now.

The Checklist

☐ Compute the annual price of your life: true monthly cost times twelve

☐ Compute the gauge: annual price times twenty-five

☐ Inventory every retirement asset by tax container: pre-tax, Roth, taxable

☐ Calculate the distance and divide it into a monthly number

☐ Automate the contribution, dated the day after payday, starting this week

The Before 40 Club Rule

Retirement is not an age. It is the day your assets can pay for your life without your hours. Hope does not fund it. Months do.

One question before you go. What is the annual price of my life, and what is it times twenty-five?

Agency: The contribution, the container mix, and the wrecker insurance are all decisions you can make now. **Urgency:** What monthly number starts this week, because the compounding cannot start without it?

Put this chapter to work in the companion Before 40 Club Workbook at before40club.com.

CHAPTER 22:

ESTATE PLANNING: DECIDING WHILE YOU ARE ALIVE

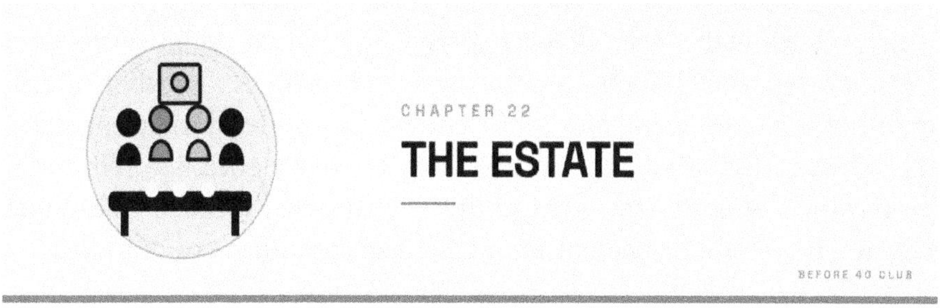

The Expensive Lesson

Everything you own is going to transfer. The only question is whether you decide how, or a court does.

That is the entire subject of estate planning, stripped of the intimidating vocabulary. It is not a rich person's topic, it is not a Q4 topic, and it is not morbid. It is the final chapter of the C.A.T. Method: you controlled the cash flow, you built the assets, you protected them from taxes, and now you decide where all of it goes and who is in charge if you cannot be. Skip this chapter and the state has a plan for you. It is called intestacy, it was written by legislators who never met your family, it runs through a public court process called probate, and it is slower, more expensive, and more public than anything you would have chosen on purpose.

Here is the pattern from eighteen years of watching what money does to grieving families. The estates that transfer clean are almost never the biggest ones. They are the documented ones: the will signed, the trust funded, the beneficiaries current, the people told. The estates that tear families apart are the silent ones, where the person who built everything never said anything, and the people left behind fill the silence with lawyers. The most expensive words in family wealth are: he never said what he wanted. This chapter exists so nobody ever says that about you.

The Story

I am going to tell you the personal version, because I lived this chapter this year. My father passed away on December 8. And before we ever needed them, my family had the documents standing: the estate plan, the will, the power of attorney, the healthcare proxy, all of it signed while he was alive and well enough to decide. We were fortunate in our bench, my background is CPA, another family member is a lawyer, my mother is a nurse, but understand clearly that the documents did the work, not the credentials. What the preparation bought us was the ability to grieve my father without also fighting a system, or each other, at the worst moment of our lives.

I have watched the other version from across the desk, and the contrast is everything this chapter claims: the unwritten wishes, the family fighting because nothing was on paper, the frozen accounts, the legal fees consuming what love built. So let me kill the myth that stops most people: you do not need to be wealthy to have a will and an estate plan. Most people do not walk around with a life plan at all, which means the moment you have one, you have an edge on most people. Having gone through this firsthand, I believe this is one of the most important chapters in the book. The documents are how you take care of your family one last time, in your own words, after your voice is gone. Mine did. Write yours.

The lesson inside every version: the documents are cheap and the silence is expensive. A basic estate plan costs less than most people's vacation. Probate, family litigation, and unplanned estate taxes cost multiples of that, paid by the people you meant to protect, at the worst moment of their lives.

What Nobody Told You

Nobody told you what a will actually does, and what it does not

A will is the base document: it names who gets what, and, if you have minor children, it names their guardian, which is reason enough to sign one this month all by itself, because without it a judge chooses. Here is what nobody explains: a will does not avoid probate. A will is instructions for probate, the public court process that validates the document, pays the debts, and distributes the rest, on the court's timeline, in the public record. A will is the floor of an estate plan, never the finish line, and dying without even the floor means intestacy: the state's default formula, distributed by statute, with a judge picking the guardian.

Nobody told you the revocable trust is the workhorse

A revocable living trust is a container you create while alive and control completely: you can change it, empty it, or cancel it any time, which is what revocable means. Assets titled into it skip probate entirely, because the trust does not die when you do. It transfers privately, quickly, and on your written terms, including terms with intelligence built in, like a child inheriting at stages instead of in one lump at eighteen. Two honest disclosures the internet skips. First, a revocable trust saves you no income or estate tax while you are alive, because you still control everything, and the plain-English tax rule of this whole chapter is: control it and it is yours, keep it and it is taxed to you. Second, an unfunded trust is a stack of paper. Funding, actually retitling the house, the accounts, the assets into the trust's name, is the step most people skip, and an unfunded trust protects no one. Signed and funded or it does not count.

Nobody told you what irrevocable actually buys, and what it costs

An irrevocable trust is the opposite trade: you genuinely give the assets up, you cannot take them back, and in exchange the assets are no longer yours, which means they can sit outside your taxable estate and, structured properly and early enough, outside the reach of certain creditors and certain long-term-care spend-down rules. This is the serious machinery: life insurance trusts that keep a large policy out of the estate, trusts that move appreciating assets out before they appreciate, planning done years before it is needed because the calendar is the whole trick. The cost is the point: irrevocable means irrevocable, and anyone who promises you control and protection from the same trust is selling something. This is the one part of the chapter that is never a form on the internet. It is a strategist, a specialist attorney, and a calendar.

Nobody told you that beneficiary designations override the will

Read that twice, because it is the most common estate mistake in America and it costs nothing to fix. Retirement accounts, life insurance, and any account with a named beneficiary transfer by that designation, directly, regardless of what the will says. The 401k from 2016 still naming an ex transfers to the ex. The will does not save it. The fix is an afternoon: pull every account, review every designation, name contingents, and put a recurring calendar reminder on it after every marriage, divorce, birth, and death. Chapter 7 told you to review beneficiaries at the merger. This chapter tells you why in bold.

Nobody told you the plan includes documents for while you are still alive

A complete plan covers incapacity, not just death: the durable power of attorney, naming who handles money if you cannot, and the healthcare proxy and living will, naming who decides and what you want when you cannot say. Without them, your family's path to helping you is a court guardianship proceeding, during a crisis, in public. These documents cost almost nothing and rescue everything.

And nobody told you the step-up, the one tax rule that changes how you hold assets for life

Under current law, many appreciated assets held until death pass to heirs with the basis stepped up to date-of-death value, which can erase decades of capital gain that a sale during life would have realized. This single rule is why sell it now versus hold it and transfer it is a real planning conversation, why gifting a highly appreciated asset during life can accidentally gift the tax bill with it, and why your estate plan and your tax plan are one plan. It is also why the T in C.A.T. does not retire when you do.

The C.A.T. Breakdown

C: Estates are cash flow events for the people left behind. Probate freezes accounts exactly when the household needs money for the funeral, the mortgage, the kids. The plan is liquidity by design: accounts that transfer instantly by designation or trust, life insurance sized to the actual obligations from Chapter 7, and a surviving spouse or family who can pay next month's bills without a court's permission. Ask one question of your current setup: if I did not come home tomorrow, what could my family access this week? If the answer is nothing, that is the assignment.

A: Everything Chapter 5 built is what this chapter titles. The A discipline is an inventory with an owner: every asset, how it is titled, where it goes, and whether the title matches the plan, because a trust that owns nothing and a will that contradicts the deeds is not a plan, it is a lawsuit kit. Business owners carry a double assignment: the succession question, who runs it, who inherits it, what the buy-sell agreement with any partner says, decided on paper while everyone is healthy, because Chapter 15 already showed you what undocumented equity does to relationships, and death is the ultimate undocumented event.

T: Estate tax has a federal exemption high enough that most families never pay it, and that is precisely how people get careless: state-level estate and inheritance taxes start much lower in some states, exemptions change with the political weather, and a business plus a house plus insurance plus accounts adds up faster than people think. The T moves live on a calendar measured in years: the annual gifting allowances used deliberately, the irrevocable structures built early for large estates, the step-up managed on purpose, the charitable pieces if giving is in your plan. And one instruction above all: your tax strategist and your estate attorney must know each other exist. Plans built in separate rooms fail in the same courtroom.

The Quarter Lens

Q1 (0 to 21): You appear in other people's documents here. If you are a parent reading this, your Q1-age children are the reason the guardianship clause exists, and naming that guardian is the single most important sentence in your entire plan.

Q2 (21 to 40): The quarter people skip, and should not. Marriage, kids, the first house, the business: every one of those Part

II exams creates an estate planning assignment the same week. The Q2 plan is simple and cheap: the will, the powers, the proxy, the beneficiary audit, and the revocable trust once real assets exist. An afternoon and a modest fee, done once, updated at life events.

Q3 (41 to 60): The upgrade quarter. Assets are now serious, the estate math is real, and the irrevocable conversations begin for larger estates, because those structures reward years and punish deathbeds. This is also the quarter you have the parent conversation, from Chapter 13, in the other direction: do your own parents have these documents, and does anyone know where they are?

Q4 (61 to 80): Maintenance and communication. The documents exist, the trust is funded, and now the family meeting happens: not the numbers necessarily, but the map, who to call, where things are, what you decided. Surprise is the enemy of every estate plan.

Overtime: The chapter after this one closes the book on what Overtime means. Here is the estate version in one line: Overtime is when the documents you signed in Q2 and Q3 finally speak, in your exact words, or the silence does.

The Move to Make Now

This week, in one sitting: the beneficiary audit. Every retirement account, every insurance policy, every account with a designation, pulled, reviewed, corrected, contingents named. It costs nothing, requires no lawyer, and fixes the most common estate disaster in the country.

This month: the floor documents. Will with guardianship if you have minors, durable power of attorney, healthcare proxy and living will. If your life is simple, this is fast. If your life has a business, real estate, or a blended family, book the estate attorney, and bring your tax strategist into the same conversation.

This quarter, if you own real assets: the revocable trust, signed and, this is the part that counts, funded. Retitle the house. Move the accounts. Signed and funded or it does not count.

Then write the map: one document, kept where your person knows, listing the accounts, the policies, the documents, the professionals, and the passwords protocol. Your family should grieve you, not excavate you.

The Warning

The warning in this chapter is the phrase I have heard from more clients than any other: we keep meaning to get to it. Estate planning is infinitely postponable because its deadline is invisible and its beneficiary is not you. So hear the actuarial truth without flinching: the documents only work if they exist before the surprise, and the surprise is called a surprise for a reason. Every year you delay, the plan you would have chosen stays unwritten, and the state's plan, the frozen accounts, the public process, the judge choosing your children's guardian, stays fully in effect, current, and ready. You are not deciding whether to have an estate plan. You have one right now. You are deciding who wrote it.

The Checklist

☐ Complete the beneficiary audit on every account and policy, contingents named

☐ Sign the will, including guardianship if you have minor children

☐ Sign the durable power of attorney and healthcare proxy and living will

☐ If real assets exist: create the revocable trust, then fund it by retitling, signed and funded

☐ Business owners: put the succession answer and any buy-sell agreement in writing

The Before 40 Club Rule

Everything you own will transfer. Decide while you are alive, in writing, or a court will decide for you, in public, at your family's expense.

One question before you go. If I did not come home tomorrow, what could my family access this week?

Agency: The beneficiary audit costs nothing and requires no lawyer. It is fully yours. **Urgency:** Which document, the will, the powers, the trust funding, gets a date this month?

Put this chapter to work in the companion Before 40 Club Workbook at before40club.com.

CHAPTER 23:

THE BEFORE 40 GAME PLAN

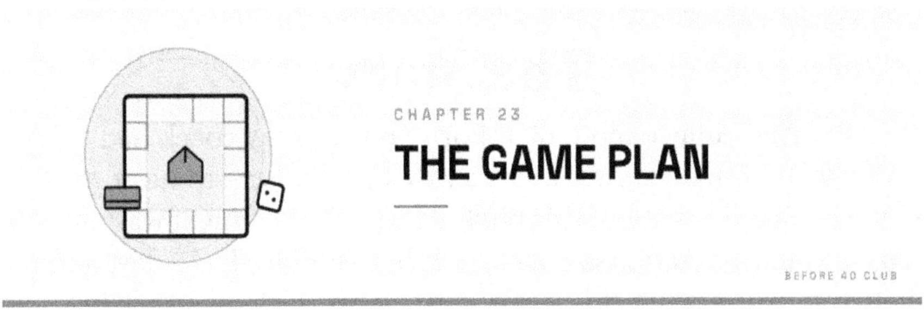

"The secret is that you have to keep going."

The Expensive Lesson

Twenty-two chapters ago, I told you nobody taught you the money game. That problem is now solved. You know the rules, the clock, the scoreboard, and the method. Which delivers you to the final expensive lesson, and it is the one I have watched cost more money than any tax mistake in this entire book:

Knowing the game is worth nothing. Playing it is worth everything, and the gap between the two is where most readers of most books go to die.

I know how this goes, because I know how it goes with everything that requires sustained execution: the reader finishes, feels genuinely changed, tells a friend about the C.A.T. thing, and then Thursday arrives, and the defaults from Chapter 2, patient, ancient, undefeated by inspiration, resume control. Six months later the book is a good memory and the return looks identical. The information was never the bottleneck. The information has never been the bottleneck. Installation is the bottleneck, and installation is not a feeling, it is a sequence: specific actions, specific order, specific dates, reviewed on a specific rhythm, until the system runs without your motivation, because your motivation was never going to last and was never supposed to.

So this final chapter is not a summary. Summaries are for people who want to remember the book. This is the Game Plan: the ninety-day installation, the annual calendar, the scoreboard, and the standing rules of the club you are now in. This is for people who want the book to have happened. Purpose comes first, the program runs on schedule, and no one, we have established twenty times, is bigger than it. Let's install.

The Story

I played college football at Fordham, and my coach had a line I have carried into every room since: we are not here to tickle you. So let me be that clear about this book. My goal in writing it was never to inspire you. Inspiration is a feeling, it burns off by Thursday, and the shelf you are reading this on is a graveyard of books that inspired people. Everybody has the knowledge now. It is free, it is everywhere, and it has never been less of an advantage. The only question left is the one this chapter asks: what are you going to do with it? Turn it into a system with dates, or carry it around as intention and read it for entertainment?

The difference has a name in my life: the installation season. It is the season you stop carrying the knowledge and start scheduling it, when the ideas stop being things you know and become recurring entries on a calendar, and the proof that mine was real is that those recurring entries still exist today, still firing, years later, long after any feeling that started them wore off. That is what I want for you, and it is the reason the book ends with ninety days of dates instead of a pep talk. The knowledge is now yours. The calendar is the test.

The distance between those two people was never discipline in the way people use that word, gritted teeth and daily willpower. It was architecture. One of them built a machine that made the right thing automatic and the review non-negotiable, and then lived a normal, distractible, human life on top of it. That is the entire promise of this chapter: you do not have to become someone else. You have to spend ninety days building the machine, and then defend a rhythm. The machine does the becoming.

What Nobody Told You

Nobody told you that ninety days installs what forty years of intention will not, so here is the sequence, in the only order that works

Days 1 to 30: the Truth phase. Everything from Part One, made physical. Week one: the scoreboard read, last year's return, thirty minutes, effective rate written down, per Chapter 1, and the C.A.T. self-grade, three letters, no inflation, worst letter circled, per Chapter 3. Week two: the money autobiography and the defaults named, three kept, three overwritten with scheduled replacements, per Chapter 2. Weeks three and four: the full truth layer, real take-home, the ninety-day spending pull, the gap computed and met, per Chapter 4, and the posture audit with the Ratmaxxing number named, per Chapter 18. Nothing in month one builds anything. Month one ends the era of not knowing, because every machine after it is sized by these numbers.

Days 31 to 60: the Pipes phase. The plumbing, installed once, running forever. The tax reserve account opened and automated on every untaxed dollar. The capture rule live: half of every future raise pre-routed to the gap. The conversion transfer: the automatic monthly investment, dated the day after payday, per Chapters 4 and 5. The estimated-payment dates calendared if you owe them, per Chapter 10. The W-4 reconciled against last April. The two-line letter protocol installed, per Chapter 11. And the protection floor from the chapters that guard everything: beneficiaries audited, the will and directives scheduled if missing, per Chapters 9 and 13. Month two is boring on purpose. Boring, automated, is the entire technology of wealth.

Days 61 to 90: the Offense phase. Now, and only now, the building. The asset thesis written and the first or next asset started, per Chapter 5. The MMM move executed, the raise conversation held or the price raised, per Chapter 16. The second-engine thesis on paper with its first customer-facing step taken. One new room entered and the deposit cadence started, three value-first gives a week, per Chapter 17. The professional bench assembled: the tax planner classified or hired, strategist not historian, per Chapter 6, and the mid-year session booked before you close this book. And the Goofball audit from Chapter 20, the ledger, the access list, the one scheduled conversation, because offense without that audit is arming the passenger.

Ninety days. None of it is heroic, most single items take under an hour, and the order is the point: truth sizes the pipes, pipes fund the offense, and offense without the first two phases is the high earner trap with enthusiasm.

Nobody told you that maintenance is a calendar, not a character trait, so here is the annual rhythm

Weekly, ten minutes, the Sunday look: accounts eyeballed, nothing decided, the habit that keeps looking neutral, per Chapter 2. Monthly, thirty minutes, the C.A.T. review: the three numbers, the gap's deployment, one letter grade rechecked, per Chapter 3. Quarterly, one hour, the operator's meeting with yourself: estimated payments if owed, the engine's revenue reviewed, one room booked, the worst letter's assignment advanced. And annually, the two fixed appointments that carry the heaviest freight: the mid-year tax planning session, June, while the year is alive, per Chapter 6, because April is too late, and the January full audit: the return read, the keep rate computed, the net worth tracked against last year, the beneficiaries checked, the Goofball ledger updated, the next year's one big move chosen. That calendar, kept, is the whole discipline. Fifty-two ten-minute looks, twelve half-hours, four hours of operating, two real sessions. Call it thirty hours a year to run your life like an owner. The Office Rat gives that to meetings about meetings every two weeks.

Nobody told you what to measure, so here is the scoreboard, five numbers, tracked yearly, on one page that becomes the most valuable document you own

The gap: real monthly in minus real monthly out, the future in installments. The keep rate: net worth against lifetime earnings, the Chapter 12 verdict. The ownership ratio: what share of your income arrives without your hours, the Chapter 5 migration, the number this whole book exists to move. The effective rate: the price you pay to play, known and bending, per Chapter 6. And the runway: months your truth layer survives at zero income, the number that buys agency. Five numbers. Not the feed's numbers, not the neighbor's, not gross income, which you now know is a headline, not a truth. When the five move right, you are winning, whatever the parking lot says.

And nobody told you that the plan must survive its author, so here is the failure protocol

You will break the rhythm. A brutal quarter, a family crisis, a season where the reviews stop and the Sunday looks lapse, it is coming, and the plan that pretends otherwise is inspiration, not architecture. The protocol: when you surface, no autopsy, no shame spiral, no starting over from day one. The pipes kept running while you were gone, that is why month two exists, so the restart is one action: hold the monthly C.A.T. review, this week, and let the rhythm resume from there. The club does not require perfection. It requires return. Stop learning money lessons the expensive way includes the lesson that quitting the whole program over a broken streak is the most expensive quit there is.

The C.A.T. Breakdown

One last time, the whole book in three letters, so you can teach it to someone, because teaching it is how you will know you own it.

C: Know your real numbers, in, out, gap. Reserve on every untaxed dollar. Pipes that run without your mood. The gap gets written assignments. Income exposes your system; the system is yours to build, and it comes first.

A: Own things that earn without your hours, business, equity, property, work that outlives the working. Start boring, start near, start survivable, start now. Hours die with the worker. The ownership ratio is the score.

T: Plan, do not just file. April is too late; June is on your calendar. The structure, not the container. The written rules, the boring middle, records that license everything. Your return is the scoreboard, and you now read it fluently.

Cash flow funds the assets. Assets multiply the cash flow. Tax planning protects both. Run the loop, in order, on your worst letter first, for the rest of your life. That is the whole religion, and you know every verse now.

The Quarter Lens

One last lap around the clock, with the Game Plan in hand.

Q1 (0 to 21): If you are reading this book in Q1, you are holding a two-decade head start almost nobody gets, and your assignment is simple: install the habits while they are free, and be in the rooms early. If you are raising someone in Q1, your household's atmosphere is their first installation. Run the plan visibly.

Q2 (21 to 40): The build quarter, and the book's namesake. Every dollar, habit, and clock started here compounds longer than it ever will again. The ninety-day install, run now, is worth multiples of the same install run later. If you are in Q2: you are not early. You are exactly on time, once.

Q3 (41 to 60): The accelerate quarter. Peak fuel meets whatever machine exists. If the machine is built, Q3 is harvest and stacking. If it is not, hear this clearly: the plan works in Q3, the sequence is identical, the runway is shorter, and the single worst move available is spending another year mourning Q2 instead of installing this quarter. Some join at 52 wishing they joined at 28. Both are welcome. Only one waited, and the waiting is over either way.

Q4 (61 to 80): The protect quarter. The plan shifts weight to T and to Chapter 13: drawdown order, structure, the transfer designed on purpose, and the discipline of helping without depleting. The five numbers still run. The rhythm still holds.

Overtime (80+): Legacy is the audit of every earlier quarter, and it is graded on organization as much as accumulation. What transfers is what was owned, documented, and discussed out loud, early. The kitchen-table meeting from Chapter 13 is Overtime's entire preparation, and it happens decades before Overtime does.

The Before 40 Club is not about your age. It never was. It is about the decision to stop learning money lessons the expensive way, and the decision is available in every quarter, today, at whatever age is reading this sentence.

Executive Time: Divide Your Days by RGA

The rhythm above tells you when to review the system. This section tells you how to run the days in between, because installation dies fastest in a calendar that treats every hour as equal.

Start with three letters that belong next to C.A.T. and MMM in your vocabulary: RGA, Revenue Generating Activities. An RGA is any task that directly creates money or directly builds an asset that will: the sales conversation, the price raise, the offer shipped, the skill practiced, the room entered, the product built, the content published that feeds the trust loop. Everything else on your list is one of two things: maintenance, the necessary upkeep that keeps the machine legal and running, the books, the emails, the errands, or theater, the Ratmaxxing from Chapter 18 wearing a to-do list costume. The exercise that changes people takes ten minutes: write down everything you did last week, then mark every line RGA, maintenance, or theater. Most people discover their week is five percent RGA, and then they stop wondering why the year did not move.

Executive Time is the fix, and it has three rules. First, RGA gets the best hours, not the leftover ones. Whatever your peak window is, and for most people it is the first two or three hours of the working day, that window is booked for RGA before anyone else can claim it, recurring, named on the calendar, defended like a client meeting, because it is one: the client is your future. Second, batch the maintenance. Maintenance expands to fill whatever it is given, so give it less: one themed block, one or two afternoons a week, where the books, the inbox, and the errands happen together and then stop. Third, delete the theater. It does not get batched. It gets named in the weekly audit and removed, and the hours go back to the first rule.

Then architect the week, not just the day. Theme your days so decisions get made once: perhaps two Offense days anchored by RGA mornings, one Maintenance day that catches everything administrative, one Rooms and content day for GAS and the trust loop, and the review rhythm from above stitched on top. The specific architecture matters less than the principle: a day with a theme starts itself, and a day without one auctions your best hours to whoever emails first. This is also how you protect founder energy, whether you are a founder or not: every decision you do not have to make about where an hour goes is energy that arrives intact at the hours that pay.

And there is a third block that outranks both, the one that gave Executive Time its name in my own calendar: protected time to think, plan, and reflect. Not producing, not maintaining, thinking. A recurring block, weekly at minimum, where the only job is to step back: what is working, what is compounding, what should stop, what does the next quarter actually require. Executives of real companies guard this time ruthlessly, and you are the executive of the company called your life. Most people never think on purpose, they only react, and every framework in this book was born in a thinking block, not a busy one. Schedule it like revenue depends on it, because it does: the RGA list itself is an output of the reflection block, and a week that starts with thinking is a week that knows where its best hours go.

One warning before the worksheet: do not confuse busy RGA with real RGA. If the activity cannot be traced to a number, a sale, a rate, an asset, an audience that feeds the funnel, it is not offense, no matter how productive it feels. The test is Chapter 16's test: can you state what it generates in one sentence with a number in it?

The Health Layer: The Asset Under Everything

One more section before the ninety days, and I am putting it here on purpose, because no game plan survives a body that cannot run it. Your health is the asset underneath every other asset in this book. Cash flow, deals, rooms, content, all of it is produced by one machine, and the machine has a maintenance schedule whether you honor it or not.

Here is my own story with it, told with the numbers, because this book only deals in numbers. During COVID I decided to get lean. The protocol was not exotic: a weight vest on my walks, fifteen thousand steps a day, and a clean diet, executed daily, the same boring repetition this entire book preaches, just applied to the body. And what I did not expect was what it did to the business. The discipline compounded sideways. My focus sharpened, my energy stabilized, my thinking blocks got deeper, and in that same lean season the firm hit its first fifty thousand dollar month, and then its first one hundred thousand dollar month. I am not telling you the steps caused the revenue. I am telling you the person who could execute the steps every single day had become the person who could execute everything else, and the body was where that person got built.

Here is what the protocol has grown into, and I share it as a practitioner, not a perfect specimen and certainly not a medical expert: at least fifteen thousand steps a day, with movement planned on the calendar instead of hoped for. Strength training, because muscle is the retirement account of the body. Swimming, and the ongoing project of learning new physical skills, because a body that keeps learning keeps working. A diet that got intentional about what and when I eat, enough water, and sleep protected like the recovery asset it is. Weight and benchmarks monitored instead of guessed at. And the unglamorous backbone: the annual physical, the bloodwork, the dental and vision visits, the age-appropriate screenings, and the numbers, blood pressure, cholesterol, blood sugar, liver health, reviewed with qualified medical professionals, because Chapter 4 taught you never to run a life on unverified numbers and your body keeps a truth layer too. Every one of those appointments and workouts sits on my calendar with the same standing as a client meeting, which is Executive Time doing its job.

Two sentences to keep from this section. Your body is the first business you are responsible for operating. And you cannot call yourself financially successful if your entire plan depends on sacrificing your health to keep earning. The full Personal Ownership Audit, covering the health, money, and life decisions you have been postponing, is waiting in the companion workbook.

So the protocol goes into the installation with everything else: the step target, the planned movement, the diet sentence you can actually keep, the protected sleep, and the appointments on the calendar. Chapter 21 already showed you bad health as the biggest retirement wrecker there is, so hear the two ends of the same truth: health protects the wealth you are building, and the discipline of health builds the person who builds the wealth. Same machine. Feed it accordingly.

The Move to Make Now

One move. Not seven. One.

Open your calendar right now, before the final pages, and schedule three things: the Day 1 scoreboard read, this week, thirty minutes, last year's return. The monthly C.A.T. review, recurring, first Sunday, thirty minutes, forever. And the June planning session, booked, even if the professional is not yet chosen, because the appointment creates the search.

Three calendar entries. Two minutes. That is the entire ask of this section, and it is deliberately small, because the reader who does the two-minute version tonight runs the ninety days, and the reader who plans to do the full version this weekend joins the inspired, and you have met their three-year results. The machine starts with an appointment. Make it, then finish the book.

The Warning

The last warning of the book belongs to the book itself.

Reading about money is a pleasure. It feels like progress, photographs like discipline, and costs nothing, which is exactly the problem: the finance-content industry, books, videos, feeds, mine included, can become one more spectator sport, one more form of Ratmaxxing, consuming the aesthetics of wealth-building while the return stays identical. You now hold enough to act for a decade. The next book, the next video, the next framework will add refinement, not readiness. You are ready. The knowledge phase of your money life is, as of this page, officially over, and everything you are tempted to consume next is either review or delay.

So here is the standard, the same one that closes every chapter because it opened your whole life: nobody taught you the money game, and that was never your fault. But nobody is coming to play it for you either. Not this book, not your planner, not the market, not luck. Nobody cares more than you will. The quarters are running. The whistle you have been waiting for blew years ago.

Welcome to the club. The dues are the ninety days. Installation starts tonight.

The Checklist

☐ Book the weekly think, plan, and reflect block, and set the daily step target with the diet sentence

☐ Join the club at before40club.com so the Scorecard, the Brief, and the community run alongside your ninety days

☐ Run the ten-minute audit: mark last week's tasks RGA, maintenance, or theater

☐ Book the recurring RGA block in your peak hours and batch maintenance into one themed slot

☐ Tonight: three calendar entries, scoreboard read this week, monthly C.A.T. review recurring, June session booked

☐ Days 1 to 30: Truth phase complete, return read, letters graded, autobiography written, truth layer built, posture audited

The Before 40 Club Rule

Knowing the game changed nothing. Playing it changes everything. Ninety days, in order, starting with tonight's calendar. The club is not something you joined. It is something you now run.

One question before you go. What date is on my ninety days, and what happens tonight?

Agency: Tonight's three calendar entries need no permission from anyone. **Urgency:** They exist before you sleep tonight, or the book stays a book.

Put this chapter to work in the companion Before 40 Club Workbook at before40club.com.

OVERTIME: THE LAST QUARTER IS DECIDED NOW

"Your life changes when your actions begin compounding in the same direction."

Every game plan ends with the clock, so let me tell you about the end of the clock, and why this chapter is short, and why it is here.

Overtime is the fifth quarter, 80 and beyond, the years past the age most financial books pretend their readers will not reach and most readers pretend not to think about. It is the quarter of legacy, the one where every account, every property, every entity, every relationship, and every silence you maintained gets its final audit, and here is the fact that justifies putting this chapter in a book called Before 40:

Overtime is the only quarter you cannot play in.

By the time it arrives, the moves are made. The step-up either protects the house or was signed away in a well-meaning transfer decades earlier. The beneficiary forms either match the family or misdirect everything to a name from another life. The documents are either findable or the estate becomes an archaeology project billed hourly. The kids either watched a system or absorbed an atmosphere of panic, and whichever one they watched is now running their households. The business either has systems that outlive the founder or it was the founder, and it ends when he does. The kitchen-table conversation either happened in a calm year or it happens now, in the worst week, between grieving people discovering each other's assumptions.

Every one of those outcomes was decided one, two, three quarters earlier, by a person who had no idea they were deciding it, or by a person who read a chapter like this one and moved. Overtime is not a quarter you play. It is a quarter you receive, and the entire question is what you shipped forward.

So this close is not new material. You already hold everything Overtime requires; it was hiding inside the chapters the whole time. The estate afternoon from Chapter 9, the will, the guardian, the beneficiaries, was an Overtime move. The kitchen-table meeting from Chapter 13, the documents located, the roles said out loud, the step-up fork run with professionals before anything moved, that was

Overtime's entire preparation, held decades early, which is the only time it can be held well. The systems conversion from Chapters 5 and 10, building things that earn and run without your hours, that was the difference between leaving assets and leaving a job that dies with you. The clean records from Chapter 6, the titled properties from Chapter 14, the tracked equity from Chapter 15: all of it was you, quietly packing the box that someone you love will one day open, in grief, hoping you were organized.

Hours die with the worker. You have known that since Chapter 5. Here is the complete version: hours die with the worker, and so do intentions, explanations, and everything you meant to get around to. What survives is what was owned, documented, structured, and said out loud, early. Assets transfer. Systems transfer. A well-installed Q1 transfers, in the habits of children who watched calm money instead of panicked money. Rooms transfer, in the doors your name still opens for people you brought along. And the method itself transfers, if you did the last item on the Chapter 23 checklist and taught it to someone, because a framework in a second head is the only inheritance that cannot be probated, taxed, or contested.

I played sports, so Overtime is not a metaphor I chose casually. Overtime is the life you were actually building the whole time, revealed. It is what you want opening the box to feel like for your family. It is what you want your name to still do in rooms you are no longer in.

My father made it close to Overtime, and he set the precedent for our family: he believed in the American dream and he built his way toward it with his own hands, business after business, and that standard now belongs to me to carry and extend. So here are the questions I am building my own Overtime against, and I am handing them to you as the last worksheet of the book. What is the standard for your future family? What reputation do you hold in your community and your circle? What have you built that your kids, your spouse, your network will still benefit from when you are not in the room? They say life is long but short, and both halves are true. My goal is for everyone reading this to make it to Overtime, and to spend the whole game looking forward to it, because that, finally, is what every framework in this book was for.

And so, the last word, and it belongs to you, whatever quarter you are standing in.

If you are in Q2: nothing in this book will ever be cheaper than it is right now. Every clock, every habit, every dollar, every room has its longest runway today. You are not early. You are exactly on time, once.

If you are in Q3: the runway is shorter and the fuel is at maximum, and the single most expensive move available to you is spending one more year grieving the quarter behind you instead of installing in the one you hold. The sequence is identical. Start tonight.

If you are in Q4: this book's weight shifts to protection and transfer, Chapters 6, 13, and this one, and your remaining moves are among the most valuable in the entire game, because they are the ones your family inherits directly. Organize, decide, and say it all out loud, this year.

And whoever you are: the ninety days from Chapter 23 are sitting on your calendar, or they are not, and that binary is the whole book now. Nobody taught you the money game. Somebody finally has. Nobody is coming to play it for you, nobody cares more than you will, no one is bigger than the program, and the program, as of this page, is yours.

Stop learning money lessons the expensive way.

The clock is running. It always was. The difference is that now, so are you.

Busayo Ogunsanya, CPA, MST Before 40 Club

JOINING THE BEFORE 40 CLUB

Here is the part where most books say thank you for reading and let you go. This book does not let you go, because the club was never a metaphor.

Membership has no fee and no form. It has behaviors. You are in the Before 40 Club the week you do these things: you run the loop, C.A.T., monthly, on your real numbers. You keep the rhythm, the weekly look, the monthly review, the June session. You work your quarter, making the moves that are cheap now instead of expensive later. And you teach the method to one person, because a framework in a second head cannot be probated, taxed, or contested, and because community does not happen accidentally. You have to foster it, and in this club the fostering is done by members, one taught person at a time.

There is one address for everything: before40club.com. Join there first, that is the move, because the Scorecard that grades your three letters lives there, the weekly Brief arrives from there, and everything the club builds next announces itself there.

Then plug into the daily feed: the videos at youtube.com/@BusayoOgunsanyaCPA, the club at instagram.com/before40club, and me at instagram.com/busayogunsanyacpa.

When a rule from this book saves you money, or a worksheet changes a decision, say so publicly: tag @busayogunsanyacpa, and leave an honest review where you bought this book, because your proof is the next member's permission, and reviews are how the club finds the people who need it.

The exams are scheduled. You now have the study guide, the workbook, and the club. Play.

APPENDIX: THE BEFORE 40 CLUB DICTIONARY

You just read a book with its own language. That was on purpose. Frameworks travel farther than paragraphs, and a saying your friend can repeat is a lesson your friend can keep. This appendix is the whole vocabulary in one place. Use it, quote it, teach it. When you share one, tag @busayogunsanyacpa so the club can find you.

The Vocabulary

The Before 40 Club. The people who decided to stop paying tuition to the expensive school. Not an age limit. A deadline mindset: learn the money game on purpose, before life grades you on it.

The C.A.T. Method. Cash Flow, Assets, Tax Planning. Cash flow funds the assets. Assets multiply the cash flow. Tax planning protects both. One engine, run in a loop, for the rest of your life.

The Money Quarters. Your money life on a game clock. Q1, ages 0 to 21: foundation, installed without your permission. Q2, 21 to 40: build, the leverage quarter. Q3, 41 to 60: accelerate. Q4, 61 to 80: protect. Overtime, 80 plus: legacy. Moves that are cheap in one quarter are expensive in the next and impossible in the one after.

The Gap. What actually comes in minus what actually goes out. Your future, arriving in monthly installments. Know it, widen it, and give every dollar of it a written job.

The Truth Layer. Your real numbers, verified against actual deposits and actual spending, instead of the gross fantasy and the budget fantasy. Everything in the method is built on it.

MMM. Make More Money. The second blade of the scissors. Defense makes money stay. Offense makes money arrive. Cutting has a floor. Earning has no ceiling. If your MMM plan cannot be stated in one sentence with a number in it, it is content, not offense.

GAS. Get Around Strangers. Your circle decides your normal. Strangers decide your next level. Opportunities travel through rooms, so get in them on purpose, give first, and never let your circle finish growing.

The Office Rat. A posture, not a job status. Waits for permission, optimizes for approval, performs effort for managers, builds nothing that belongs to him. Both the Rat and the Owner can collect a W-2. Same desk, two postures, two futures.

Ratmaxxing. The performance mode of the Office Rat: visible effort, fake urgency, meetings about meetings, busy theater that builds nothing you own.

The Owner. The other posture. Moves without permission, optimizes for equity, treats the employer as the largest client and the paycheck as runway, and owns something that earns without hours.

The Goofball. The most expensive person in your financial life, and he has your face. The ego purchases, the avoided conversations, the wrong circle kept too long. The goofball rides for life. Your job is to make sure he never drives again.

The Goofball Filter. One question, run on every person with access to you: does this person make me sharper, calmer, or better resourced, or make me spend, doubt, and perform? Expand aggressively. Admit selectively.

Lovable Liabilities. What children are, said with all the love in the world. Most kids will not be LeBron James. They will be wonderful, expensive, and dependent on your planning for a long time, which is why the planning starts before the birth.

The Hope Plan. The most popular retirement strategy in America: a feeling instead of a number. Hope is what people call the absence of a plan when they need to change the subject.

The Exam Days. Marriage. The house. The kids. The business. The IRS letter. Life moments that are secretly money exams, graded on preparation you did months or years earlier. The exams are scheduled. This book is the study guide.

The Capture Rule. Half of every raise and bonus goes to the gap, permanently, before the lifestyle finds it.

The Oxygen Mask Rule. Retirement funding before college funding, your own boat before the rescue. Your child can borrow for school. You cannot borrow for your sixties.

Pattern Recognition. The builder's trade: facts, then patterns, then insights, then strategy, then execution. Many people collect facts. Fewer recognize patterns. The pay rises at every rung, because the crowd thins.

Distribution Is the Moat. Products get copied. Distribution compounds. The formula: pattern recognition to repeatable workflow to embedded distribution to recurring revenue to proprietary data to stronger product.

Embedded Distribution. The richest question in building: how can customers receive your product as part of something they are already doing? When you are a step inside someone else's workflow, every new customer gets cheaper.

Work With the Willing. Build with, sell to, and learn from the people already in motion. Chasing skeptics is the highest customer acquisition cost you will ever pay, billed in energy. Willingness is the qualification. Everything else is teachable.

RGA. Revenue Generating Activities. Any task that directly creates money or directly builds an asset that will. Everything else is maintenance or theater. Most people's week is five percent RGA, and that number, not talent, is why the year does not move.

Executive Time. RGA gets the best hours, maintenance gets batched, theater gets deleted. Theme the days so decisions get made once, because a day without a theme auctions your best hours to whoever emails first.

April Is the Autopsy. Filing is recording history. Planning is writing it. Every option that could have changed the number died on December 31.

The Compounding Laws

The club's second vocabulary: the operating lines. Same rules apply. Use them, quote them, tag @busayogunsanyacpa.

Agency compounds. Excuses do not. Every act of moving without permission makes the next one easier. Every excuse does the same for the next excuse. Both are flywheels. Pick which one you feed.

The Money Ladder. The first $1,000 comes from work. The first $100,000 comes from skill. The first $1 million comes from systems. People stall when they try to climb the next rung with the last rung's tool.

You do not get paid for potential. You get paid for execution. Potential is the most overvalued asset in the world because its owner does all the valuing.

Compound your own effort. Stop trying to compound other people's effort. A career built entirely on someone else's flywheel spins their wheel. Create momentum where you have ownership.

The Compounding Four. Your identity, your relationships, your systems, and your distribution all compound. So do status, proof, and trust. Everything on that list is buildable on purpose, and almost nobody builds them on purpose.

The Trust Loop. Content creates trust. Trust creates customers. Customers create proof. Proof creates better content. Every business with an audience runs this loop, knowingly or not.

The Flywheel Rule. The flywheel starts with one move, but every move makes the next one easier. The first video, the first client, the first asset, the first room: all disproportionately hard, all disproportionately important.

Agency and Urgency. Agency says, I can do something about this. Urgency says, I should not keep waiting. Agency without urgency becomes potential. Urgency without agency becomes anxiety. You need both.

Curate or Be Curated. If you do not curate your life, your obligations, distractions, habits, and other people's priorities will curate it for you. The calendar, the cash flow, the health, the relationships, the weekends, the future: all being curated right now, by you or by default.

Day One thinking. Operate like the story is just starting, because the moment you decide it is finished, it is.

Do not let someone else's pace become your bottleneck. Waiting on the slow partner, the hesitant client, the skeptical relative is a tax on your compounding. Work with the willing and keep moving.

Never let the universe smooth you into your surroundings. The world will make you average if you let it, quietly, one reasonable compromise at a time. The whole club exists to interrupt that process.

The 23 Rules

One rule per chapter. Every one of them fits on a sticky note, and every one of them was paid for by somebody.

1. Nobody Taught You The Money Game. The game does not care whether you know the rules. Learn them anyway, because the tuition for guessing never stops billing.

2. The Q1 Audit: Where Your Money Defaults Came From. Your defaults were installed without your permission. They only keep running with it.

3. The C.A.T. Method. Cash flow funds the assets. Assets multiply the cash flow. Tax planning protects both. Run the loop or the loop runs you.

4. Cash Flow: The Truth Layer. Your gap is your future arriving in monthly installments. Know it, widen it, and give every dollar of it a written job.

5. Assets: Stop Renting Out Your Hours. Hours die with the worker. Own something that works when you do not, and start while it is still embarrassing.

6. Tax Planning: April Is Too Late. Filing records history. Planning writes it. Be the person whose April is a formality.

7. Before You Get Married. The wedding is one day. The merger is the rest of your life. Plan them in that proportion.

8. Before You Buy The House. The bank tells you the max. The truth layer tells you the number. Never confuse the ceiling for the plan.

9. Before You Have Kids. Fund their future without unfunding yours. The account is a gift. The atmosphere is the inheritance.

10. Before You Start The Business. The entity is a container. The strategy is what you run inside it. Stop framing the certificate and start feeding the system.

11. Before You Ignore The IRS Letter. The letter is a number wearing a costume. Open it, read the code, run the four checks, and take the costume off.

12. The High Earner Trap. Income is the flow. Wealth is what stayed. You are not what you make. You are what you kept.

13. Before You Help Family With Money. Structure is not the opposite of love. Structure is how love survives money. Decide everything early, out loud, on paper.

14. Before You Buy The Rental. Buy the spreadsheet, not the story. The code rewards landlords who read the rules before the closing, and invoices everyone else.

15. Before You Take Or Give Equity. In equity, the paperwork is the strategy. The exit is decided at the entrance, and the clocks only start for people who start them.

16. MMM: Make More Money. Cutting has a floor. Earning has no ceiling. Sharpen both blades, and run every new dollar through the pipes.

17. GAS: Get Around Strangers. Opportunities travel through rooms. Get around strangers on purpose, give first, filter hard, and never let your circle finish growing.

18. The Office Rat And The Owner. Nobody is coming to promote you into your own life. Same desk, two postures, two futures. Move like the Owner, in order, starting now.

19. The Builder: From Patterns To Platforms. Facts are free. Judgment gets paid. See the pattern, build the workflow, embed the distribution, and work with the willing.

20. The Goofball Chapter. The goofball rides for life. Your job is not to kill him. Your job is to make sure he never drives again.

21. Retirement: The Hope Plan And The C.A.T. Plan. Retirement is not an age. It is the day your assets can pay for your life without your hours. Hope does not fund it. Months do.

22. Estate Planning: Deciding While You Are Alive. Everything you own will transfer. Decide while you are alive, in writing, or a court will decide for you, in public, at your family's expense.

23. The Before 40 Game Plan. Knowing the game changed nothing. Playing it changes everything. Ninety days, in order, starting with tonight's calendar. The club is not something you joined. It is something you now run.

Share the one that cost you the most. Tag @busayogunsanyacpa.

ABOUT THE AUTHOR

Busayo Ogunsanya is a Certified Public Accountant with a Master of Science in Taxation from Fordham University and 18 years across tax, accounting, startups, and real client money problems. He has spent his career reading the actual tax returns of high earners and business owners, the documents where financial lives tell the truth, and turning what those returns reveal into plain-language strategy.

His work and commentary have appeared in The Wall Street Journal, Forbes, and Crain's New York Business.

He is the founder of BigApple Accounting CPA, a New York based firm serving business owners and high earners, the co-founder of Muse Tax, a Techstars company delivering AI tax insights through the payroll companies and banks businesses already use, and the creator of the Before 40 Club, the C.A.T. Method, and the Money Quarters framework you just read. His entire body of work runs on one conviction: nobody should have to learn money lessons the expensive way when somebody who reads the returns for a living is willing to just tell you.

He lives and works in New York City.

Take the next step. The fastest way to find out what your own numbers are trying to tell you is a conversation, and everything starts at one address: before40club.com.

Where to Find Me

Join the club: before40club.com
The firm, for tax and advisory work: bigappleaccountingcpa.com
YouTube: youtube.com/@BusayoOgunsanyaCPA
Instagram: instagram.com/busayogunsanyacpa
Club Instagram: instagram.com/before40club

The companion Before 40 Club Workbook, with the full exercises, assessments, quizzes, Scoreboard, and 90-Day Tracker for all 23 chapters, is available on Amazon and at before40club.com.

New videos every week on tax strategy, cash flow, buying a home, business ownership, and the real-life money decisions this book runs on. Subscribe on YouTube and the next lesson finds you.

www.ingramcontent.com/pod-product-compliance
Lightning Source LLC
LaVergne TN
LVHW010717061126
851857LV00014B/1230
* 9 7 9 8 2 5 6 2 7 7 4 3 7 *